P9-ELR-564

KEEP
CALM
AND
VEG(ETARIAN)

KEEP
CALM

AND

VEG(ETARIAN)

THUNDER BAY
P · R · E · S · S

Thunder Bay Press
An imprint of the Baker & Taylor Publishing Group
10350 Barnes Canyon Road, San Diego, CA 92121
www.thunderbaybooks.com

Copyright © 2014 The National Magazine Company Limited and Collins & Brown

Produced by Collins & Brown
an imprint of Anova Books Company Ltd.,
10 Southcombe Street, London W14 0RA, U.K.

Copyright under International, Pan American, and Universal Copyright Conventions. All rights reserved. No part of this book may be reproduced or transmitted in any form or by any means, electronic or mechanical, including photocopying, recording, or by any information storage-and-retrieval system, without written permission from the copyright holder. Brief passages (not to exceed 1,000 words) may be quoted for reviews.

"Thunder Bay" is a registered trademark of Baker & Taylor. All rights reserved.

All notations of errors or omissions should be addressed to Thunder Bay Press, Editorial Department, at the above address. All other correspondence (author inquiries, permissions) concerning the content of this book should be addressed to Collins & Brown Old Magistrates Court, 10 Southcombe Street, London, W14 0RA, U.K.

ISBN-13: 978-1-60710-927-3
ISBN-10: 1-60710-927-1

Library of Congress Cataloging-in-Publication Data

Dixon, Barbara (Barbara Elizabeth)
  Keep calm and veg(etarian) / Barbara Dixon.
    pages cm
  ISBN 978-1-60710-927-3 -- ISBN 1-60710-927-1
  1. Vegetarian cooking. I. Title.
  TX837.D55 2013
  641.5'636--dc23
                          2013024472

Printed in China

1 2 3 4 5 17 16 15 14 13

Cover illustration by Emma Kelly

Photographers: Neil Barclay (pages 53, 55, 58, 138, and 171); Martin Brigdale (pages 48, 65, 86, 87, 94, 105, 119, and 120); Nicki Dowey (pages 9, 12, 15, 17, 18, 19, 21, 22, 27, 28, 31, 33, 34, 37, 38, 40, 42, 47, 52, 57, 61, 63, 69, 73, 74, 77, 78, 81, 84, 88, 91, 99, 100, 102, 103, 109, 112, 115, 125, 126, 127, 131, 134, 137, 147, 151, 152, 153, 155, 156, 161, 162, 167, 168, 173, 174, 176, 182, 187, 191, 194, 205, 207, 208, 211, 215, 216, 217, 220, 223, 224, 227, 228, 232, and 235); Will Heap (pages 66, 97, 116, 158, and 175); Craig Robertson (pages 13, 25 41, 46, 51, 75, 82, 83, 106, 107, 111, 113, 139, 144, 145, 148, 149, 159, 179, 183, 188, 193, 197, 199, 200, and 203); Lucinda Symons (pages 11, 39, 128, 132, 141, 180, and 231)

Home Economists: Anna Burges-Lumsden, Joanna Farrow, Emma Jane Frost, Teresa Goldfinch, Alice Hart, Lucy McKelvie, Kim Morphew, Katie Rogers, Bridget Sargeson, Sarah Tildesley, and Jennifer White

Stylists: Lucy McKelvie, Wei Tang, Sarah Tildesley, Helen Trent, Fanny Ward, and Mari Mererid Williams

Notes
All spoon measures are level.
1 teaspoon = 5ml spoon; 1 tablespoon = 15ml spoon.
Ovens and broilers must be preheated to the specified temperature.
Large eggs should be used except where otherwise specified.

Dietary Guidelines
Note that certain recipes contain raw or lightly cooked eggs. The young, elderly, pregnant women, and anyone with immune-deficiency disease should avoid these because of the slight risk of salmonella.
Note that some recipes contain alcohol. Check the ingredients list before serving to children.

Contents

SOUPS AND SALADS

Beet Soup

Preparation Time 15 minutes • Cooking Time 40–45 minutes • Serves 8 • Per Serving 216 calories, 9g fat (3g saturated), 31g carbohydrates, 1,500mg sodium • Gluten Free • Easy

1 tablespoon olive oil

1 onion, finely chopped

9 beets (about 1¾ pounds), peeled and cut into ½-inch cubes

2 red-skinned or white round potatoes, peeled and coarsely chopped

4 cups hot vegetable stock

juice of 1 lemon

½ cup sour cream

2 ounces mixed root vegetable chips

salt and ground black pepper

2 tablespoons chopped chives to garnish

1. Heat the oil in a large saucepan, add the onion, and cook over medium heat for 5 minutes. Add the beets and potatoes, and cook for another 5 minutes.

2. Add the hot stock and lemon juice, and then bring to a boil. Season with salt and black pepper, reduce the heat, and simmer, covering with a lid halfway, for 25 minutes. Cool slightly. Then puree in a blender until smooth.

3. Pour the soup into a clean saucepan and reheat gently. Divide the soup among eight warmed bowls. Add 1 tablespoon sour cream to each bowl, sprinkle with black pepper, top with a few vegetable chips, and sprinkle the chopped chives on top to serve.

FREEZING TIP

To freeze *Complete the recipe to the end of step 2. Freeze the soup in a sealed container. It will keep for up to three months.*

To use *Thaw in the refrigerator overnight. Reheat gently and simmer over low heat for 5 minutes.*

Bloody Mary Soup with Toasted Bread

Preparation Time 15 minutes, plus marinating and chilling • Cooking Time 5 minutes • Serves 4 •
Per Serving 468 calories, 23g fat (4g saturated), 52g carbohydrates, 1,500mg sodium • Dairy Free • Easy

**11 ripe plum tomatoes (about
1½ pounds), thinly sliced**
**6 scallions, trimmed and
finely chopped**
grated zest of ½ lemon
**2 tablespoons freshly chopped
basil, plus extra basil leaves
to garnish**
**½ cup extra virgin olive oil, plus
extra to drizzle**
2 tablespoons balsamic vinegar
2–3 garlic cloves, crushed
a pinch of sugar
¼ cup chilled vodka*
**1 tablespoon vegetarian
Worcestershire sauce**
a few drops of Tabasco
⅔ cup tomato juice
**8 thin slices French or Italian
bread**
salt and ground black pepper

1. Put the tomatoes into a large shallow dish and sprinkle with the scallions, lemon zest, and basil.

2. Blend together the oil, vinegar, 1 crushed garlic clove, the sugar, vodka, Worcestershire sauce, and Tabasco. Season to taste with salt and black pepper, and pour the marinade over the tomatoes. Cover and let marinate for 2 hours at room temperature.

3. Put the tomato mixture and tomato juice into a blender and blend until smooth. Transfer to a bowl and let chill in the refrigerator for 1 hour.

4. Just before serving, preheat the broiler. Put the bread on the broiler rack and toast lightly on both sides. Rub each one with the remaining crushed garlic, drizzle with oil, and garnish with fresh basil leaves. Spoon the soup into bowls, drizzle with oil, sprinkle with black pepper, and serve at once with the bread.

This recipe is not suitable for children because it contains alcohol.

Fava Bean, Pea, and Mint Soup

Preparation Time 20 minutes • Cooking Time 30 minutes • Serves 4 •
Per Serving 176 calories, 4g fat (1g saturated), 22g carbohydrates, 100mg sodium • Easy

1 tablespoon olive oil
1 medium onion, finely chopped
2½ cups shelled fresh fava beans
 (about 2½ pounds unshelled)
1½ cups shelled fresh peas (about
 1½ pounds unshelled)
4½ cups hot vegetable stock
2 tablespoons freshly chopped
 mint, plus extra leaves to
 garnish
3 tablespoons crème fraîche, plus
 extra to garnish (optional)
salt and ground black pepper

1. Heat the oil in a large saucepan and sauté the onion gently for 15 minutes, until softened.

2. Meanwhile, blanch the fava beans by cooking them for 2–3 minutes in a large pot of boiling water. Drain and refresh under cold water. Slip the beans out of their skins.

3. Put the beans and peas into the pot with the onion and stir for 1 minute. Add the hot stock and bring to a boil. Simmer for 5–8 minutes, until the vegetables are tender. Then cool for a few minutes. Stir in the mint, and then blend in batches in a blender until smooth. Alternatively, use an immersion blender.

4. Return the soup to the rinsed-out pot, stir in the crème fraîche, and check the seasoning. Reheat gently. Ladle into warmed bowls, and garnish with a little crème fraîche, if desired, and mint leaves.

Sweet Potato Soup

Preparation Time 20 minutes • Cooking Time 40 minutes • Serves 8 • Per Serving 78 calories, 2g fat (trace saturated), 14g carbohydrates, 800mg sodium • Gluten Free • Dairy Free • Easy

1 tablespoon olive oil
1 large onion, finely chopped
2 teaspoons coriander seeds, crushed
2 fresh red chilies, seeded and chopped (see Cook's Tip)
1 butternut squash, peeled and coarsely chopped
2 sweet potatoes, coarsely chopped
2 tomatoes, peeled and diced
7 cups hot vegetable stock
salt and ground black pepper

1. Heat the oil in a large saucepan over gentle heat and sauté the onion for about 15 minutes, until soft. Add the coriander seeds and chilies to the pan and cook for 1–2 minutes.

2. Add the squash, sweet potatoes, and tomatoes and cook for 5 minutes. Add the hot stock, cover, and bring to a boil. Simmer gently for 15 minutes or until the vegetables are soft. Using a blender, puree the soup in batches until smooth. Season with salt and black pepper.

3. Return the soup to the pot. Reheat gently, and then divide among eight warmed bowls. Sprinkle with black pepper.

COOK'S TIP
Chilies vary greatly in strength, from mild to blisteringly hot, depending on the type of chili and its ripeness. Taste a small piece first to check that the chilies are not too hot for you.

When handling chilies, be careful not to touch or rub your eyes with your fingers, because they will sting. Wash knives immediately after handling chilies. As a precaution, use rubber gloves when preparing them, if desired.

Pasta and Chickpea Soup with Pesto

Preparation Time 25 minutes • Cooking Time about 1 hour • Serves 6 • Per serving 211 calories, 8g fat (1g saturated), 26g carbohydrates, 300mg sodium • Easy

3 tablespoons olive oil

1 onion, chopped

2 garlic cloves, finely chopped

1 small leek, trimmed and sliced

1 teaspoon freshly chopped
   rosemary

1 (15-ounce) can chickpeas

5 cups vegetable stock

4 ripe tomatoes, skinned and
   chopped

1 zucchini, diced

¾ cup shelled peas

1 cup green beans, halved

¾ cup fava beans, shelled

2 ounces dried pastina (small
   soup pasta)

2 tablespoons freshly chopped
   parsley

salt and ground black pepper

pesto (see **Cook's Tip**) and freshly
   grated pecorino or Parmesan
   cheese (see **Cook's Tip** on
   page 18) to serve

1. Heat the oil in a large saucepan, add the onion, garlic, leek, and rosemary, and sauté gently for 5–6 minutes, until softened but not browned. Add the chickpeas with their liquid, the stock, and the tomatoes. Bring to a boil. Then reduce the heat, cover the pan, and simmer for 40 minutes.

2. Add the zucchini, peas, green beans, and fava beans. Return to a boil. Then reduce the heat and simmer for 10 minutes. Add the pasta and parsley and simmer for 6–8 minutes, until al dente. Season to taste with salt and black pepper.

3. Ladle into warmed bowls and serve topped with a spoonful of pesto and a sprinkling of cheese.

COOK'S TIP

Pesto

Put 3 cups freshly chopped basil, ½ cup grated Parmesan, 2 tablespoons pine nuts, and ½ crushed garlic clove into a food processor. With the motor running, add ¼–⅓ cup extra virgin olive oil to make a paste. Season well with salt and black pepper.

Green Lentil and Coconut Soup

Preparation Time 20 minutes • Cooking Time 40 minutes • Serves 4 • Per Serving 442 calories, 22g fat (10g saturated), 48g carbohydrates, 300mg sodium • Dairy Free • Easy

1 cup whole green lentils
¼ cup sunflower oil
3 red-skinned or white round
    potatoes, peeled and diced
1 large onion, chopped
2 garlic cloves, crushed
¼ teaspoon ground turmeric
2 teaspoons ground cumin
⅔ cup dried coconut
3¼ cups vegetable stock
1¼ cups coconut milk
finely grated zest of 1 lemon, plus
    extra to garnish
salt and ground black pepper
toasted fresh coconut to garnish

1. Put the lentils into a strainer and wash thoroughly under cold running water. Drain well.

2. Heat the oil in a large saucepan. Add the potatoes and sauté gently for 5 minutes, until they begin to brown. Remove with a slotted spoon and drain on paper towels.

3. Add the onion to the pan and sauté gently for 10 minutes, until soft. Add the garlic, turmeric, and cumin, and sauté for 2–3 minutes. Add the coconut, stock, coconut milk, and lentils, and bring to a boil. Then reduce the heat, cover, and simmer gently for 20 minutes or until the lentils are just tender.

4. Add the potatoes and lemon zest, and season to taste with salt and black pepper. Cook gently for another 5 minutes or until the potatoes are tender. Ladle into warmed bowls, garnish with toasted coconut and lemon zest, if desired, and serve hot.

Zucchini and Leek Soup

Preparation Time 15 minutes • Cooking Time 35–40 minutes • Serves 8 • Per Serving 246 calories, 9g fat (3g saturated), 32g carbohydrates, 100mg sodium • Easy

1 tablespoon olive oil
1 onion, finely chopped
2 leeks, trimmed and sliced
6 zucchini (about 2 pounds), grated
5½ cups hot vegetable stock
4 short rosemary sprigs
1 small loaf French bread
1¼ cups Gruyère cheese,
shredded (see Cook's Tip)
salt and ground black pepper

1. Heat the oil in a large saucepan. Add the onion and leeks, and cook for 5–10 minutes. Add the zucchini and cook, stirring, for another 5 minutes.

2. Add the hot stock and 3 rosemary sprigs, and then bring to a boil. Season with salt and black pepper, reduce the heat, and simmer for 20 minutes.

3. Preheat the broiler to medium-high. Slice the bread into eight pieces, and broil for 1–2 minutes on one side, until golden. Turn the bread over, sprinkle with cheese, and season. Broil for another 1–2 minutes. Keep the croûtes warm.

4. Let the soup cool a little. Remove the rosemary sprigs and blend the soup in batches in a blender or food processor until smooth. Pour into a clean stockpot and reheat gently.

5. Ladle into warmed bowls, garnish with the croûtes, and sprinkle with the remaining rosemary leaves.

COOK'S TIP

Vegetarian cheeses Some vegetarians prefer to avoid cheeses that have been produced by the traditional method, because this uses animal-derived rennet. Some supermarkets and cheese shops now stock vegetarian cheeses, produced using vegetarian rennet.

Spicy Bean and Zucchini Soup

Preparation Time 10 minutes • Cooking Time 30 minutes • Serves 4 • Per Serving 289 calories, 8g fat (1g saturated), 43g carbohydrates, 1,500mg sodium • Dairy Free • Easy

2 tablespoons olive oil
1 medium onion, finely chopped
2 garlic cloves, crushed
2 teaspoons ground coriander
1 tablespoon paprika
1 teaspoon mild curry powder
3 zucchini, halved lengthwise,
  and sliced (see Cook's Tip)
2 red-skinned or white round
  potatoes, peeled and diced
1 (15-ounce) can red kidney beans,
  drained and rinsed
1 (15-ounce) can great Northern
  beans, drained and rinsed
6⅓ cups vegetable stock
salt and ground black pepper
crusty bread to serve

1. Heat the oil in a large saucepan. Add the onions and garlic, and sauté for 2 minutes. Add the spices and cook, stirring, for 1 minute. Mix in the zucchini and potatoes and cook for 1–2 minutes.

2. Add the remaining ingredients and bring to a boil. Then reduce the heat, cover the pan, and simmer for 25 minutes, stirring occasionally, or until the potatoes are tender. Adjust the seasoning if necessary.

3. Ladle into warmed bowls and serve with crusty bread.

COOK'S TIP
Look for medium, firm zucchini. They lose their flavor as they grow.

Pumpkin and Butternut Squash Soup

Preparation Time 20 minutes • Cooking Time 40 minutes • Serves 4 • Per Serving 398 calories,
32.5g fat (21g saturated), 19g carbohydrates, 800mg sodium • Easy

**1 butternut squash, peeled,
  seeded, and coarsely diced**
**8 cups pumpkin (or use another
  butternut squash), peeled,
  seeded, and diced**
¾ cup coarsely chopped shallots
1 fat garlic clove, chopped
**1 teaspoon coriander seeds,
  crushed**
½ cup (1 stick) butter, melted
2½ cups vegetable stock
2½ cups full-fat milk
salt and ground black pepper
**fresh basil sprigs and sour cream
  to garnish**
crusty bread to serve

1. Preheat the oven to 425°F. Put the squash, pumpkin, shallots, garlic, and coriander seeds into a large roasting pan and toss with the melted butter. Season the vegetables well with salt and black pepper and bake for about 30 minutes, until golden brown and just cooked through.

2. Meanwhile, in a saucepan, heat the stock and milk.

3. Transfer the vegetables to a large saucepan. Pour the hot stock into the roasting pan and stir to loosen the remaining sediment in the pan. Add this to the vegetables in the saucepan, and then stir in the milk.

4. Put three-quarters of the soup into a blender or food processor and blend until smooth. Mash the remaining soup mixture. Then stir the two together and reheat gently. Ladle into warmed bowls, garnish with basil and swirls of sour cream, and serve with crusty bread.

Spring Vegetable Broth

Preparation Time 20 minutes • Cooking Time 20 minutes • Serves 4 • Per Serving 264 calories, 6g fat (3g saturated), 35g carbohydrates, 2,400mg sodium • Easy

1 tablespoon olive oil

4 shallots, chopped

1 fennel bulb, chopped

1 leek, trimmed and chopped

5 small carrots, chopped

4½ cups hot vegetable stock

2 zucchini, chopped

1 bunch of asparagus, chopped

2 (15-ounce) cans cannellini beans, drained and rinsed

2 ounces Gruyère or Parmesan cheese shavings (see Cook's Tip on page 18) to serve

1. Heat the oil in a large saucepan. Add the shallots, fennel, leek, and carrots, and sauté for 5 minutes or until they start to soften.

2. Add the hot stock, cover, and bring to a boil. Add the zucchini, asparagus, and beans. Then reduce the heat and simmer for 5–6 minutes, until the vegetables are tender.

3. Ladle into warmed bowls, sprinkle with cheese, and serve.

TRY SOMETHING DIFFERENT

This broth is also good with a tablespoon of pesto (see Cook's Tip on page 14) added to each bowl, and served with crusty bread.

Tomato, Mozzarella, and Red Pesto Salad

Preparation Time 10 minutes • Serves 4 • Per Serving 400 calories, 36g fat (12g saturated), 3g carbohydrates, 2,900mg sodium • Gluten Free • Easy

1½ cups baby plum tomatoes, halved

8 ounces mozzarella balls, drained (see Cook's Tip)

⅓ cup sun-dried tomato pesto

1 cup ripe black olives, drained and pitted

3½ cups mixed salad greens

salt and ground black pepper

1. Put the tomatoes, mozzarella, pesto, and olives into a large bowl and toss together. Season with black pepper. The olives are already salty so check the seasoning before adding any salt. Cover the bowl and put to one side.

2. Just before serving, toss the salad greens with the tomato and mozzarella mixture.

COOK'S TIP

If you can't find mozzarella balls, buy larger mozzarella instead and cut it into large cubes.

– cut back tom. pesto

Sprouted Bean Trio and Mango Salad

Preparation Time 15 minutes • Serves 6 • Per Serving 103 calories, 4g fat (1g saturated), 15g carbohydrates, 100mg sodium • Dairy Free • Easy

3 tablespoons mango chutney

grated zest and juice of 1 lime

2 tablespoons olive oil

4 plum tomatoes

1 small red onion, finely chopped

1 red bell pepper, seeded and finely diced

1 yellow bell pepper, seeded and finely diced

1 mango, peeled, pitted, and finely diced

¼ cup freshly chopped cilantro

4½ cups sprouted bean trio (such as lentil, mung, and adzuki)

salt and ground black pepper

1. To make the dressing, put the mango chutney into a small bowl and add the lime zest and juice. Whisk in the oil, and season with salt and black pepper.

2. Quarter the tomatoes, discard the seeds, and then dice. Put into a large bowl with the onion, bell peppers, mango, cilantro, and bean sprouts. Pour in the dressing and mix well. Serve immediately.

TRY SOMETHING DIFFERENT

Use papaya instead of mango.

Ginger and Chili Dressing

Mix together 2 teaspoons grated fresh ginger, 1 tablespoon sweet chili sauce, 2 teaspoons white wine vinegar, and 2 tablespoons walnut oil. Season with salt.

Peanut Dressing

Mix together 1 tablespoon peanut butter, ¼ of a whole dried chili, crushed, 4 teaspoons white wine vinegar, 3 tablespoons walnut oil, 1 teaspoon sesame oil, and a dash of soy sauce.

Endive, Blue Cheese, and Walnut Salad

Preparation Time 15 minutes • Cooking Time 5 minutes • Serves 4 • Per Serving 270 calories, 24g fat (12g saturated), 5g carbohydrates, 800mg sodium • Gluten Free • Easy

7 ounces Stilton or other blue cheese, crumbled (see Cook's Tip on page 18)
⅓ cup heavy cream
nutmeg to grate
2 teaspoons milk
2 Pippin apples, cored and sliced
juice of ½ lemon
1 head each green and red endive, trimmed and leaves separated
3 handfuls of mixed salad greens
½ cup walnuts, toasted
salt and ground black pepper

1. Put 4 ounces of the blue cheese into a saucepan with the cream and a grating of nutmeg. Stir over gentle heat until simmering. If too thick, add a little milk at a time until it's the consistency of a creamy dressing.

2. Toss the apples and the lemon juice in a bowl. Add the endives to the bowl with the mixed salad greens. Season with salt and black pepper and toss. Divide among four plates, along with the toasted walnuts and remaining blue cheese. Drizzle the dressing over the salad and serve immediately.

GET AHEAD
To prepare ahead Complete the recipe to the end of step 1 up to one day in advance and keep chilled.

To use Reheat the cheese sauce gently just before serving. Complete the recipe.

Panzanella

Preparation Time 20 minutes, plus chilling • Serves 4 • Per Serving 228 calories, 14g fat (3g saturated), 21g carbohydrates, 600mg sodium • Easy

2–3 thick slices from a day-old country loaf, torn or cut into cubes

4 ripe tomatoes, coarsely chopped

2 tablespoons capers

1 teaspoon freshly chopped thyme

1 small red onion, thinly sliced

2 garlic cloves, finely chopped

2 small red chilies, seeded and finely chopped (see Cook's Tip on page 13)

¼ cup extra virgin olive oil

¾ cup ripe black olives, pitted

1 cup sun-dried tomatoes, coarsely chopped

8 fresh basil leaves

1 ounce Parmesan cheese shavings (see Cook's Tip on page 18)

salt and ground black pepper

fresh thyme sprigs to garnish

1. Put the bread into a large bowl with the tomatoes, capers, thyme, onion, garlic, chilies, oil, olives, and sun-dried tomatoes. Season well with salt and black pepper. Toss together and let sit in a cool place for at least 30 minutes.

2. Toss the salad thoroughly again. Tear the basil into pieces and sprinkle them over the salad with the Parmesan shavings. Garnish with thyme sprigs and serve.

GET AHEAD

This salad is best made 2–3 hours ahead to the let the flavors mingle.

Ciabatta and Mozzarella Salad

Preparation Time 10 minutes • Cooking Time 5 minutes • Serves 4 • Per Serving 613 calories, 33g fat (13g saturated), 56g carbohydrates, 2,400mg sodium • Easy

8 thick slices Italian bread, such as ciabatta

2 teaspoons olive paste (tapenade) or sun-dried tomato paste

11 ounces mozzarella cheese, drained and sliced (see Cook's Tip on page 18)

¼ cup olive oil, plus extra to drizzle

2 tablespoons balsamic vinegar

12 marinated artichoke hearts in oil, drained and sliced (see Cook's Tip)

3½ cups arugula

1 cup sun-dried tomatoes, halved

salt and ground black pepper

1. Preheat the broiler. Toast the bread slices on one side for 1–2 minutes. Spread the untoasted side with olive or sun-dried tomato paste. Top with mozzarella slices and drizzle lightly with oil.

2. Mix the vinegar, salt, and black pepper in a bowl and whisk in the oil. Add the artichoke hearts.

3. Place the bread slices back under the broiler for 2–3 minutes, until the mozzarella browns lightly.

4. Toss the arugula with the artichoke mixture and divide among four plates. Top with two slices of broiled bread and the sun-dried tomatoes and serve.

COOK'S TIP

Find marinated artichokes in supermarkets; alternatively, buy canned artichoke hearts, drain, slice, and cover in olive oil. They will keep in the refrigerator for up to one week.

Feta, Peach, and Arugula Salad

Preparation Time 15 minutes • Cooking Time 10 minutes • Serves 6 • Per Serving 271 calories, 22g fat (7g saturated), 10g carbohydrates, 1,400mg sodium • Easy

3 slices walnut bread, cubed
1 tablespoon olive oil
4 peaches, halved, pitted,
    and cut into wedges
2 cups mixed salad greens
2 cups arugula
7 ounces feta cheese, coarsely
    broken up (see Cook's Tip on
    page 18)
¼ cup each walnuts and mixed
    seeds and nuts (such as
    flaxseeds, pine nuts, and
    sesame seeds)
1 tablespoon toasted sesame oil
3 tablespoons extra virgin olive oil
2 tablespoons red wine vinegar
a few fresh mint leaves, chopped
salt and ground black pepper
1 lemon, cut into 6 wedges,
    to serve

1. Preheat the oven to 400°F. Put the cubed bread on a baking sheet, drizzle with the olive oil, and bake for 10 minutes until golden brown. Put the peaches into a large bowl with the mixed salad, arugula, feta, and nuts and seeds.

2. Mix together the sesame and extra virgin olive oils and the vinegar, add the mint leaves, and season with salt and black pepper. Add half of the dressing to the bowl and toss together.

3. Divide the salad among six plates, and then drizzle with the remaining dressing. Serve each with a lemon wedge to squeeze over the salad.

yummy

Roasted Root Vegetable Salad

Preparation Time 20 minutes, plus cooling • Cooking Time 40 minutes • Serves 4 • Per Serving 290 calories, 14g fat (2g saturated), 33g carbohydrates, 700mg sodium • Gluten Free • Dairy Free • Easy

1 butternut squash, halved, seeded, and cubed

1½ large carrots, cut into chunks

3 fresh thyme sprigs

1½ tablespoons olive oil

2 red onions, cut into wedges

1 tablespoon balsamic vinegar

1 (15-ounce) can chickpeas, drained and rinsed

¼ cup pine nuts, toasted

3½ cups arugula

salt and ground black pepper

yummy

* cook veg. in iron skillet instead

* heat pine nuts in a dry hot skillet 5-8 min. + or - to toast

1. Preheat the oven to 375°F. Put the squash and carrots into a large, deep roasting pan. Sprinkle the thyme sprigs over them, drizzle with 1 tablespoon oil, and season with salt and black pepper. Roast for 20 minutes.

2. Take the pan out of the oven, give it a good shake to make sure the vegetables aren't sticking, and then add the onions. Drizzle the remaining oil over the vegetables and toss to coat. Roast for another 20 minutes or until all the vegetables are tender.

3. Remove the roasted vegetables from the oven and discard any twiggy sprigs of thyme. Drizzle the vinegar over the top, stir in, and let cool.

4. To serve, put the chickpeas into a large serving bowl. Add the cooled vegetables, the pine nuts, and arugula (saving a few leaves for the garnish). Toss everything together and garnish with the reserved arugula leaves.

GET AHEAD

To prepare ahead *Complete the recipe to the end of step 3. Then cool, cover, and chill for up to two days.*

To use *Complete the recipe.*

Spinach and Carrot Salad

Preparation Time 5 minutes • Cooking Time 4 minutes • Serves 4 • Per Serving 173 calories, 12g fat (2g saturated), 12g carbohydrates, 800mg sodium • Gluten Free • Dairy Free • Easy

4 carrots, sliced
8 ounces green beans, trimmed
1 (12-ounce) package baby spinach
1 garlic clove, crushed
2 teaspoons soy sauce
2 teaspoons honey
1 tablespoon cider vinegar
¼ cup olive oil
ground black pepper

1. Cook the carrots in lightly salted boiling water for 3–4 minutes, adding the beans for the last minute. Drain and rinse in cold water. Drain well, and then put both in a bowl with the spinach.

2. Put the garlic into a small bowl. Add the soy sauce, honey, vinegar, and oil. Season with black pepper and whisk together thoroughly. Pour some of the dressing over the carrot, bean, and spinach mixture, and toss together well. Serve the remaining dressing separately.

TRY SOMETHING DIFFERENT
Add a handful of raisins or lightly toasted sesame seeds.

Winter Leaf Salad

Preparation Time 10 minutes • Serves 4 • Per Serving 196 calories, 20g fat (2g saturated),
2g carbohydrates, 600mg sodium • Gluten Free • Dairy Free • Easy

2 tablespoons white wine vinegar

2 tablespoons walnut oil

¼ cup olive oil

3 cups mâche

1 small head radicchio

2 small heads red endives

**¾ cup walnuts, toasted
   and coarsely chopped**

salt and ground black pepper

1. Put the white wine vinegar, walnut oil, and olive oil into a jar with a lid. Season with salt and black pepper, and shake well to mix.

2. Tear the salad greens into bite-size pieces and put into a large bowl. Add the walnuts and toss to mix together.

3. To serve, shake the dressing again, and then pour it over the salad and toss well.

TRY SOMETHING DIFFERENT

Add orange segments for a really refreshing salad.

Winter Slaw

Preparation Time 15 minutes • Serves 4 • Per Serving 265 calories, 10g fat (1g saturated), 38g carbohydrates, 400mg sodium • Gluten Free • Dairy Free • Easy

4 oranges
1 (15-ounce) can chickpeas,
   drained and rinsed
8 carrots (about 1 pound), shredded
½ red cabbage (about 1¼ pounds),
   finely shredded
½ cup golden raisins
⅓ cup freshly chopped cilantro
¼ cup extra virgin olive oil
3 tablespoons red wine vinegar
salt and ground black pepper

1. Using a sharp knife, cut a thin slice of peel and pith from each end of the oranges. Put the oranges, cut side down, on a board and cut off the peel and pith. Remove any remaining pith. Cut out each segment, leaving the membrane behind. Squeeze the juice from the membrane into a bowl.

2. Put the orange segments and juice into a serving bowl with the chickpeas, carrots, cabbage, golden raisins, and cilantro. Add the oil and vinegar and season well with salt and black pepper.

3. Toss everything together to coat thoroughly.

GET AHEAD
To prepare ahead *Complete the recipe. Store the coleslaw in a sealable container in the refrigerator for up to two days.*

Warm Tofu, Fennel, and Bean Salad

Preparation Time 10 minutes • Cooking Time 15 minutes • Serves 4 • Per Serving 150 calories, 6g fat (1g saturated), 15g carbohydrates, 800mg sodium • Gluten Free • Dairy Free • Easy

- **1 tablespoon olive oil, plus 1 teaspoon**
- **1 red onion, finely sliced**
- **1 fennel bulb, finely sliced**
- **1 tablespoon cider vinegar**
- **1 (15-ounce) can lima beans, drained and rinsed**
- **2 tablespoons freshly chopped Italian parsley**
- **7 ounces smoked tofu**
- **salt and ground black pepper**

1. Heat 1 tablespoon oil in a large skillet. Add the onion and fennel, and cook over medium heat for 5–10 minutes, until soft.

2. Add the vinegar and heat through for 2 minutes. Stir in the lima beans and parsley, season with salt and black pepper, and then transfer to a bowl.

3. Slice the smoked tofu horizontally into four and then into eight triangles. Add them to the skillet with the remaining teaspoon of oil. Cook for 2 minutes on each side or until golden brown.

4. Divide the bean mixture among four plates, and add two slices of tofu to each plate.

Warm Pear and Walnut Caesar Salad

Preparation Time 10 minutes • Cooking Time 5 minutes • Serves 6 • Per Serving 397 calories, 31g fat (8g fat saturated), 19g carbohydrates, 1,300mg sodium • Easy

Excellent!

½ cup walnut pieces

1 tablespoon walnut or mild olive oil

2 teaspoons butter

3 firm Comice pears, quartered, cored, and thickly sliced

1 (12-ounce) bag Caesar salad with croutons, dressing, and Parmesan (see Cook's Tip on page 18)

3½ ounces blue cheese, such as Roquefort, Stilton, or Danish blue, crumbled

1 bunch of fresh chives, coarsely chopped

1. Put the walnuts into a nonstick skillet and dry-fry over medium heat for about 1 minute, until lightly toasted. Set aside.

2. Heat the oil and butter in the skillet, and then add the pears. Sauté for 2 minutes on each side or until golden brown. Remove with a slotted spoon.

3. To serve, put the salad greens into a large bowl. Add the walnuts, pears, croutons, Parmesan, and blue cheese. Add the salad dressing and toss lightly, or serve the dressing separately in a small bowl. Serve immediately, garnished with chives.

GET AHEAD

To prepare ahead Complete the recipe to the end of step 2. Then let the pears sit in the skillet and set aside for up to 4 hours.
To use Warm the pears in the skillet for 1 minute, and then complete the recipe.

LIGHT BITES
AND SNACKS

Tomato Crostini with Feta and Basil

Preparation Time 20 minutes • Cooking Time 3 minutes • Serves 4 • Per Serving 242 calories, 17g fat (3g saturated), 18g carbohydrates, 1,500mg sodium • Easy

1 small garlic clove, crushed
3 tablespoons freshly chopped basil, plus extra basil leaves to garnish
¼ cup pine nuts
2 tablespoons extra virgin olive oil
grated zest and juice of 1 lime
2 ounces feta cheese (see Cook's Tip on page 18)
1 tablespoon water
4 large ripe tomatoes, thickly sliced
½ cup fresh tomato salsa (see Cook's Tip)
¼ cup ripe black olives, pitted and coarsely chopped
4 thick slices country-style bread

1. Put the garlic, chopped basil, pine nuts, oil, lime zest, and juice into a food processor and process to a smooth paste. Add the feta cheese and process until smooth. If necessary, thin with 1 tablespoon water. Season with salt and black pepper.

2. Put the tomatoes, salsa, and olives into a bowl and gently toss together.

3. Toast the bread. Divide the tomato mixture among the slices of toast and spoon the basil and feta mixture on top. Garnish with basil leaves and serve.

COOK'S TIP
Salsa
Put ½ ripe avocado, peeled, pitted, and coarsely chopped, 4 coarsely chopped tomatoes, 1 teaspoon olive oil, and the juice of ½ lime into a bowl and stir well. Serve at once.

Beefsteak Tomatoes with Bulgur

Preparation Time 10 minutes • Cooking Time 30–35 minutes • Serves 4 • Per Serving 245 calories, 14g fat (4g saturated), 21g carbohydrates, 700mg sodium • Easy

1 cup bulgur wheat

3 ounces feta cheese, chopped (see Cook's Tip on page 18)

1 zucchini, chopped

½ cup Italian parsley, finely chopped

½ cup slivered almonds, toasted

4 large beefsteak tomatoes

1 tablespoon olive oil

1. Preheat the oven to 350°F. Cook the bulgur according to the package directions. Chop the feta and zucchini and stir into the bulgur with the parsley and almonds.

2. Chop the top off each tomato and scoop out the seeds. Put on a baking sheet and spoon in the bulgur mixture. Drizzle with oil and cook in the oven for 15–20 minutes, until the cheese starts to soften. Serve immediately.

TRY SOMETHING DIFFERENT

Try quinoa instead of the bulgur wheat. Put the quinoa in a bowl of cold water and mix well, and then soak for 2 minutes. Drain. Put into a saucepan with twice its volume of water and bring to a boil. Simmer for 20 minutes. Remove from the heat, cover, and let stand for 10 minutes.

Roast Mushrooms with Cashew Nuts

Preparation Time 5 minutes • Cooking Time 5–8 minutes • Serves 4 • Per Serving 75 calories, 6g fat (1g saturated), 2g carbohydrates, 100mg sodium • Gluten Free • Easy

1 tablespoon vegetable oil
2 tablespoons unsalted cashew
   nuts
8 ounces brown-cap mushrooms,
   sliced
1 tablespoon lemon juice
¼ cup freshly chopped cilantro,
   plus fresh sprigs to garnish
1 tablespoon light cream or soy
   cream (optional)
salt and ground black pepper

1. Heat the oil in a wok or large skillet. Add the cashew nuts and cook over high heat for 2–3 minutes, until golden brown. Add the mushrooms and cook for another 2–3 minutes until tender, stirring frequently.

2. Stir in the lemon juice and cilantro, and season to taste with salt and black pepper. Heat until bubbling. Remove the skillet from the heat and stir in the cream. Adjust the seasoning as needed and serve immediately, garnished with cilantro sprigs.

TRY SOMETHING DIFFERENT
Chinese Garlic Mushrooms
Replace the nuts with 2 crushed garlic cloves and stir-fry for only 20 seconds before adding the mushrooms. Replace the lemon juice with rice wine or dry sherry. This recipe is not suitable for children because it contains alcohol.

Mozzarella Mushrooms

Preparation Time 2–3 minutes • Cooking Time 15–20 minutes • Serves 4 • Per Serving 137 calories, 9g fat (5g saturated), 5g carbohydrates, 400mg sodium • Easy

8 large portabello mushrooms
8 slices marinated red bell pepper
8 fresh basil leaves
5 ounces mozzarella cheese, cut into eight slices (see Cook's Tip on page 18)
2 English muffins, halved
salt and ground black pepper
green salad to serve

1. Preheat the oven to 400°F. Lay the mushrooms side by side in a roasting pan and season with salt and black pepper. Top each mushroom with a slice of red bell pepper and a basil leaf. Lay a slice of mozzarella on top of each mushroom and season again. Roast in the oven for 15–20 minutes, until the mushrooms are tender and the cheese has melted.

2. Meanwhile, toast the English muffin halves until golden. Put a mozzarella mushroom on top of each muffin half. Serve immediately with a green salad.

Red Onions with Rosemary Dressing

Preparation Time 20 minutes • Cooking Time 30–35 minutes • Serves 8 • Per Serving 91 calories,
6g fat (trace saturated), 9g carbohydrates, trace sodium • Gluten Free • Dairy Free • Easy

**3 large red onions, root intact,
each cut into eight wedges**
⅓ cup olive oil
¼ cup balsamic vinegar
**2 teaspoons freshly chopped
rosemary**
salt and ground black pepper

1. Preheat the barbecue grill. Soak eight wooden skewers in water for 20 minutes. Thread the onion wedges onto the skewers. Brush with about 3 tablespoons oil, and then season well with salt and black pepper.

2. Barbecue the onion kebabs for 30–35 minutes, turning from time to time and brushing with oil when necessary, until tender and lightly charred.

3. To make the dressing, mix the vinegar with the remaining oil and the rosemary. Drizzle the rosemary dressing over the cooked onions and serve.

Chili Onions with Goat Cheese

Preparation Time 15 minutes • Cooking Time 45 minutes • Serves 4 • Per Serving 276 calories,
23g fat (16g saturated), 5g carbohydrates, 900mg sodium • Gluten Free • Easy

6 tablespoons unsalted butter, softened
2 medium red chilies, seeded and finely chopped (see Cook's Tip on page 13)
1 teaspoon crushed red pepper flakes
6 small red onions
3 (3½-ounce) goat cheese logs, with rind (see Cook's Tip on page 18)
salt and ground black pepper
balsamic vinegar to serve

1. Preheat the oven to 400°F. Put the butter into a small bowl, beat in the fresh chili and red pepper flakes, and season well with salt and black pepper.

2. Cut off the root from one of the onions, sit it on the bottom, and then make several deep cuts in the top to create a star shape, slicing about two-thirds of the way down the onion. Do the same with the other five onions. Then divide the chili butter equally among them, pushing it down into the cuts.

3. Put the onions into a small roasting pan, cover with aluminum foil, and bake for 40–45 minutes, until soft.

4. About 5 minutes before the onions are ready, slice each goat cheese in two, leaving the rind intact. Then put on a baking sheet and bake for 2–3 minutes.

5. To serve, put each onion on top of a piece of goat cheese and drizzle with balsamic vinegar.

Hash Browns with Fried Eggs

Preparation Time 20 minutes, plus cooling • Cooking Time 20–25 minutes • Serves 4 • Per Serving 324 calories, 16g fat (7g saturated), 36g carbohydrates, 400mg sodium • Gluten Free • Easy

8 russet potatoes (about 2 pounds), scrubbed and left whole

3 tablespoons butter

4 extra-large eggs

salt and ground black pepper

sprigs of fresh Italian parsley to garnish

1. Put the potatoes into a large saucepan of cold water. Cover, bring to a boil, and parboil for 5–8 minutes. Drain and let cool for 15 minutes.

2. Preheat the oven to 300°F. Put a baking sheet inside to warm. Peel the potatoes and coarsely shred them lengthwise into long strands. Divide into eight portions and shape into mounds.

3. Melt half the butter in a large nonstick skillet. When it begins to brown, add four of the potato mounds, spacing them well apart, and flatten them a little. Pan-fry slowly for 6–7 minutes, until golden brown. Then turn them and brown the other side for 6–7 minutes. Transfer to the warmed baking sheet and keep warm in the oven while you pan-fry the rest.

4. Just before serving, carefully break the eggs into the hot skillet and cook for about 2 minutes, until the white is set and the yolk is still soft. Season with salt and black pepper, and serve with the hash browns. Garnish with parsley.

Spicy Bean and Tomato Fajitas

Preparation Time 15 minutes • Cooking Time 25 minutes • Serves 6 • Per Serving 512 calories, 20g fat (6g saturated), 71g carbohydrates, 1,500mg sodium • Easy

2 tablespoons sunflower oil

1 onion, sliced

2 garlic cloves, crushed

½ teaspoon hot chili powder, plus extra to garnish

1 teaspoon each ground coriander and ground cumin

1 tablespoon tomato paste

1 (14½-ounce) can diced tomatoes

1 cup canned red kidney beans, drained and rinsed

1 (15-ounce) can cranberry beans, drained and rinsed

1 (15-ounce) can great Northern beans, drained and rinsed

⅔ cup hot vegetable stock

2 ripe avocados

juice of ½ lime

1 tablespoon freshly chopped cilantro, plus sprigs to garnish

6 flour tortillas

⅔ cup sour cream

salt and ground black pepper

lime wedges to serve

1. Heat the oil in a large skillet, add the onion, and cook gently for 5 minutes. Add the garlic and spices and cook for another 2 minutes.

2. Add the tomato paste and cook for 1 minute. Then add the tomatoes, beans, and hot stock. Season well with salt and black pepper and bring to a boil. Then reduce the heat and simmer for 15 minutes, stirring occasionally.

3. Halve, pit, peel, and chop the avocados. Put the avocado into a bowl, add the lime juice and chopped cilantro, and mash. Season to taste.

4. Warm the tortillas. Either wrap them in aluminum foil and heat in the oven at 350°F for 10 minutes, or put onto a plate and microwave on full power for 45 seconds (based on a 900W oven).

5. Spoon some beans down the center of each tortilla. Fold up the bottom to keep the filling inside, and then wrap the sides in so they overlap. Spoon the avocado and sour cream over the fajitas. Sprinkle with chili powder and cilantro sprigs and serve with lime wedges.

Falafel, Arugula, and Sour Cream Wraps

Preparation Time 5 minutes, plus chilling • Serves 6 • Per Serving 270 calories, 9g fat (4g saturated), 42g carbohydrates, 500mg sodium • Easy

6 large flour tortillas

¾ cup sour cream

3½ cups arugula

¼ cup fresh cilantro, chopped

1 celery stick, finely chopped

1 (6½-ounce) package falafel mix, prepared according to package directions and coarsely chopped or crumbled

1. Lay the tortillas on a board and spread each one with sour cream.

2. Divide the arugula among the wraps and sprinkle with cilantro, celery, and falafel.

3. Roll the tortillas up as tightly as you can. Then wrap each roll in plastic wrap and chill for up to 3 hours or until ready to use. To serve, unwrap and cut each roll into quarters.

Veggie Pitas

Preparation Time 8 minutes • Serves 1 • Per Serving 322 calories, 11g fat (2g saturated), 47g carbohydrates, 1,200mg sodium • Easy

4 whole-wheat pita breads
4 tablespoons hummus (see page 67), plus extra to serve
½ cup unsalted cashew nuts
8 cremini mushrooms, finely sliced
1 cucumber, chopped
fresh mixed salad greens
ground black pepper

1. Split the pita breads and spread with the hummus.

2. Fill the pitas with the cashew nuts, mushrooms, cucumber, and a generous helping of salad greens. Serve with extra hummus, if desired, and season with black pepper.

TRY SOMETHING DIFFERENT
Add a diced ripe avocado. It is rich in omega fats and good for your skin.

Chickpea Cakes

Preparation Time 20 minutes, plus chilling • Cooking Time about 15 minutes • Serves 4 •
Per Serving 344 calories, 17g fat (2g saturated), 37g carbohydrates, 1,000mg sodium • Dairy Free • Easy

**2 (15-ounce) cans chickpeas,
   drained and rinsed
4 garlic cloves, crushed
1 teaspoon ground cumin
1 small red onion, chopped
¾ cup fresh cilantro
2 tablespoons all-purpose flour,
   plus extra to dust
olive oil for pan-frying
mixed salad and lemon wedges
   to serve**

1. Pat the chickpeas dry with paper towels. Then put them into a food processor with the garlic, cumin, onion, and cilantro. Process until smooth, and then stir in the flour.

2. With floured hands, shape the chickpea mixture into 12 small, round patty-shaped cakes and chill in the refrigerator for 20 minutes.

3. Heat a little oil in a nonstick skillet over medium heat and pan-fry the cakes in batches for about 2 minutes on each side or until heated through and golden brown. Serve warm with mixed salad and lemon wedges.

FREEZING TIP

To freeze *Make the cakes, and then cool, put in a freezerproof container, and freeze. They will keep for up to one month.*
To use *Thaw overnight at a cool room temperature, and then reheat in the oven at 350°F for 20 minutes.*

Vegetable Tempura

Preparation Time 20 minutes • Cooking Time 15 minutes • Serves 4 • Per Serving 450 calories,
21g fat (3g saturated), 55g carbohydrates, 2,100mg sodium • Dairy Free • A Little Effort

**1 cup all-purpose flour, plus
2 tablespoons extra to sprinkle**

2 tablespoons cornstarch

2 tablespoons arrowroot

1¼ cups ice-cold water

1 cup small cauliflower florets

**2 large carrots, cut into
matchsticks**

16 white mushrooms

2 zucchini, sliced

**2 red bell peppers, seeded and
sliced**

vegetable oil for deep-frying

salt and ground black pepper

fresh cilantro sprigs to garnish

FOR THE DIPPING SAUCE

**¾-inch piece fresh ginger, peeled
and grated**

¼ cup dry sherry*

3 tablespoons soy sauce

¾ cup boiling water

1. Sift the flour, cornstarch, and arrowroot into a large bowl with a pinch each of salt and black pepper. Gradually whisk in the water to form a thin batter. Cover and chill.

2. To make the dipping sauce, put the ginger, sherry, and soy sauce into a heatproof bowl and pour in the water. Stir well to mix, and then put aside.

3. Put the vegetables into a large bowl and sprinkle with the 2 tablespoons flour. Toss well to coat. Heat the oil in a wok or deep-fryer to about 350°F. (Test by frying a small cube of bread; it should brown in 40 seconds.)

4. Dip a handful of the vegetables in the batter. Then remove with a slotted spoon, taking up a lot of the batter with the vegetables. Add to the hot oil and deep-fry for 3–5 minutes, until crisp and golden. Remove with a slotted spoon and drain on paper towels; keep them hot while you cook the remaining batches. Serve immediately, garnished with cilantro sprigs and accompanied by the dipping sauce.

** The dipping sauce is not
suitable for children because it
contains alcohol.*

Lemon Hummus with Black Olives

Preparation Time 15 minutes • Serves 4 • Per Serving 284 calories, 16g fat (2g saturated), 25g carbohydrates, 1,200mg sodium • Gluten Free • Dairy Free • Easy

2 (15-ounce) cans chickpeas, drained and rinsed
1 garlic clove, crushed (use fresh garlic when possible, see Cook's Tip)
grated zest and juice of 1 lemon
¼ cup olive oil
1–2 tablespoons cold water
2 tablespoons ripe black olives, pitted and coarsely chopped
1 teaspoon paprika, plus a little extra to sprinkle (optional)
sticks of raw vegetables and breadsticks to serve

1. Put the chickpeas and garlic into a food processor, add the lemon zest and juice, and process to combine. With the motor running, drizzle the oil into the machine to make a thick paste. If the hummus is too thick, add the water and process again.

2. Spoon into a bowl and stir in the olives and paprika. Sprinkle with a little extra paprika, if desired, and serve with raw vegetables and breadsticks for dipping.

COOK'S TIP

Raw garlic is renowned for its curative and protective powers, which include lowering blood pressure and cholesterol levels.

Fresh garlic has juicy mild cloves and is available throughout the summer. It is the classic form of garlic to use for making dishes such as pesto, salsa verde, garlic mayonnaise, and chilled soups.

Cheese Scone Twists

Preparation Time 15 minutes • Cooking Time 12 minutes • Makes 14 • Per Serving 193 calories,
8g fat (5g saturated), 26g carbohydrates, 600mg sodium • Easy

6 tablespoons butter, plus extra to grease
3¼ cups all-purpose flour, plus extra to dust
5 teaspoons baking powder
1¼ cups shredded sharp cheddar (see Cook's Tip on page 18)
about 1¼ cups milk, plus extra to glaze
a pinch of salt

1. Preheat the oven to 425°F. Lightly grease two (or three) baking sheets. Sift together the flour, baking powder, and a pinch of salt into a bowl, and then rub in the butter. Add half of the cheese and stir in enough milk to make a soft, but not sticky, dough. Knead briefly to bring together.

2. Roll out on a floured work surface to a thickness of ½ inch. Cut out circles with a 3-inch cutter and remove the centers using a 1½-inch cutter.

3. Lightly knead the trimmings, including the 1½-inch circles, and roll out again. Cut out more rings until all the dough is used.

4. Twist each ring to form a figure eight and space well apart on the baking sheets. Brush with milk and sprinkle with the remaining cheese. Bake for about 12 minutes, until well risen and golden brown. Let cool on a wire rack.

TRY SOMETHING DIFFERENT
Add a pinch of cayenne pepper to the flour in step 1 and sprinkle with ¼ cup Parmesan cheese in step 4.

VEGETABLE
MAINS

Grilled Vegetables with Walnut Sauce

Preparation Time 25 minutes • Cooking Time 15–20 minutes • Serves 4 • Per Serving 598 calories,
48g fat (6g saturated), 35g carbohydrates, 300mg sodium • Dairy Free • Easy

2 large carrots, peeled and cut into
   ¼-inch slices
1 fennel bulb, thinly sliced
1 large sweet potato, thinly sliced
8 ounces Jerusalem artichokes,
   scrubbed and thinly sliced
8 ounces thick asparagus
   spears, trimmed
8 baby leeks, trimmed
¼–⅓ cup olive oil
salt and ground black pepper

FOR THE WALNUT SAUCE
2 slices day-old bread,
   crusts removed
2 tablespoons water
¾ cup walnuts, toasted
2 garlic cloves, chopped
1 tablespoon red wine vinegar
2 tablespoons freshly chopped
   parsley
⅓ cup olive oil
¼ cup walnut oil

1. First make the walnut sauce. Crumble the bread into a bowl, add the water, and then squeeze dry. Put the bread into a food processor with the toasted walnuts, garlic, vinegar, and parsley, and process until fairly smooth. Add the olive and walnut oils and process briefly to form a thick sauce. Season with salt and black pepper and transfer to a serving dish.

2. Preheat the broiler to medium-high. Baste the vegetables with the oil and broil in batches, turning once, for 2–6 minutes, until charred and tender (see Cook's Tip). Keep warm in a low oven while broiling the rest.

3. Transfer all the broiled vegetables to a warmed serving plate and season with a little salt and black pepper. Serve with the walnut sauce.

COOK'S TIP
The root vegetables take longest to cook through, while the asparagus and leeks need only a short time under the broiler.

Spicy Roasted Roots

Preparation Time 25 minutes • Cooking Time about 1½ hours • Serves 8 • Per Serving 134 calories,
8g fat (1g saturated), 14g carbohydrates, 100mg sodium • Gluten Free • Dairy Free • Easy

3 carrots, sliced lengthwise
3 parsnips, sliced lengthwise
3 tablespoons olive oil
1 butternut squash, peeled,
    seeded, and chopped
2 red onions, cut into wedges
2 leeks, sliced
3 garlic cloves, roughly chopped
2 tablespoons mild curry paste
    (see Cook's Tip on page 83)
salt and ground black pepper

1. Preheat the oven to 400°F. Put the carrots and parsnips into a large roasting pan, drizzle with 1 tablespoon oil, and cook for 40 minutes.

2. Add the butternut squash, onions, leeks, and garlic to the roasting pan. Season with salt and black pepper. Then drizzle with the remaining 2 tablespoons oil.

3. Roast for 45 minutes, until the vegetables are tender and golden brown. Stir in the curry paste and return to the oven for another 10 minutes. Serve immediately.

FREEZING TIP
To freeze *Complete the recipe, and then cool, wrap, and freeze for up to one month.*
To use *Thaw overnight at room temperature, and then reheat at 400°F for 20 minutes in an ovenproof dish with ¾ cup hot stock.*

Roasted Ratatouille

Preparation Time 15 minutes • Cooking Time about 1½ hours • Serves 6 • Per Serving 224 calories, 18g fat (3g saturated), 14g carbohydrates, trace sodium • Gluten Free • Dairy Free • Easy

4 red bell peppers, seeded and coarsely chopped
1 large eggplant, stem removed and cut into chunks
3 onions, peeled and cut into wedges
4 or 5 garlic cloves, unpeeled and left whole
⅔ cup olive oil
1 teaspoon fennel seeds
¾ cup canned tomato puree or tomato sauce
sea salt and ground black pepper
a few fresh thyme sprigs to garnish

1. Preheat the oven to 475°F. Put the bell peppers, eggplant, onions, garlic, oil, and fennel seeds into a roasting pan. Season with sea salt flakes and black pepper, and toss.

2. Transfer to the oven and bake for 30 minutes (tossing frequently during cooking) or until the vegetables are charred and begin to soften.

3. Stir the tomato puree or sauce through the vegetables and put the roasting pan back in the oven for 50–60 minutes, stirring occasionally. Garnish with the thyme sprigs and serve.

TRY SOMETHING DIFFERENT
Replace half the eggplant with 3 zucchini; use a mixture of green and red bell peppers; garnish with fresh basil instead of thyme.

Squash with Chickpeas

Preparation Time 15 minutes • Cooking Time 25–30 minutes • Serves 6 • Per Serving 228 calories, 12g fat (2g saturated), 22g carbohydrates, 600mg sodium • Gluten Free • Dairy Free • Easy

1 squash (such as butternut, acorn, or kabocha [see Cook's Tip]), peeled, seeded, and chopped into ¾-inch cubes
1 garlic clove, crushed
2 tablespoons olive oil
2 (15-ounce) cans chickpeas, drained and rinsed
⅔ cup water
½ red onion, thinly sliced
1 large bunch of fresh cilantro, coarsely chopped
salt and ground black pepper
steamed spinach to serve

FOR THE TAHINI SAUCE
1 large garlic clove, crushed
3 tablespoons tahini paste
juice of 1 lemon
¼ – ⅓ cup cold water

1. Preheat the oven to 425°F. Toss the squash in the garlic and oil, and season. Put into a roasting pan and roast for 25 minutes or until soft.

2. Meanwhile, put the chickpeas and water into a saucepan over medium heat and warm through.

3. To make the tahini sauce, put the garlic into a bowl, add a pinch of salt, and then whisk in the tahini paste. Add the lemon juice and cold water—enough to make a consistency somewhere between light and heavy cream—and season.

4. Drain the chickpeas and put them into a large bowl. Then add the roasted squash, onion, and cilantro. Pour the tahini sauce over them and toss carefully. Adjust the seasoning and serve while warm, with spinach.

COOK'S TIP
Kabocha is a Japanese variety of winter squash and has a dull-colored deep green skin with whitish stripes. Its flesh is an intense yellow-orange.

Leek and Broccoli Bake

Preparation Time 20 minutes • Cooking Time 45–55 minutes • Serves 4 • Per Serving 245 calories, 13g fat (4g saturated), 18g carbohydrates, 400mg sodium • Gluten Free • Easy

2 tablespoons olive oil
1 large red onion, cut into wedges
1 eggplant, chopped
2 leeks, trimmed and cut into chunks
1 broccoli head, cut into florets and stalks chopped
3 large flat mushrooms, chopped
5½ cups cherry tomatoes (about 1¾ pounds)
3 fresh rosemary sprigs, chopped
1¼ cups boiling water
½ cup freshly grated Parmesan cheese (see Cook's Tip on page 18)
salt and ground black pepper

1. Preheat the oven to 400°F. Heat the oil in a large flameproof dish, add the onion, eggplant, and leeks, and cook for 10–12 minutes, until golden and softened.

2. Add the broccoli, mushrooms, cherry tomatoes, half the rosemary, and the boiling water. Season with salt and black pepper. Stir well, cover, and bake in the oven for 30 minutes.

3. Meanwhile, put the Parmesan into a bowl. Add the remaining rosemary and season with black pepper. When the vegetables are cooked, remove the lid and sprinkle the Parmesan mixture on top. Cook, uncovered, in the oven for another 5–10 minutes, until the topping is golden brown.

TRY SOMETHING DIFFERENT
Use sliced zucchini instead of eggplant.

Spring Vegetable Stew

Preparation Time 20 minutes • Cooking Time 30–35 minutes • Serves 4 • Per Serving 270 calories, 17g fat (10g saturated), 23g carbohydrates, 600mg sodium • Gluten Free • Dairy Free • Easy

8 ounces new potatoes, scrubbed

6 tablespoons unsalted butter

4 shallots, blanched in boiling water, drained, peeled, and thinly sliced

1 garlic clove, crushed

2 teaspoons freshly chopped thyme

1 teaspoon grated lime zest

6 baby leeks, trimmed and sliced into 2-inch lengths

12 baby carrots, scrubbed

¾ cup shelled peas

¾ cup shelled fava beans

1¼ cups vegetable stock

1 Boston lettuce, shredded

¼ cup freshly chopped mixed herbs, such as chervil, chives, mint, and parsley

salt and ground black pepper

1. Put the potatoes into a saucepan of lightly salted water. Bring to a boil, cover, and parboil for 5 minutes. Drain and refresh under cold water.

2. Meanwhile, melt half the butter in a large sauté pan, add the shallots, garlic, thyme, and lime zest, and sauté gently for 5 minutes or until softened and lightly golden brown. Add the leeks and carrots and sauté for another 5 minutes. Stir in the potatoes, peas, and fava beans. Then pour in the stock and bring to a boil. Reduce the heat, cover the pan, and simmer gently for 10 minutes. Remove the lid and cook, uncovered, for another 5–8 minutes, until all the vegetables are tender.

3. Add the shredded lettuce to the stew with the chopped herbs and remaining butter. Heat through until the butter is melted. Check the seasoning and serve.

Tomato and Lima Bean Stew

Preparation Time 10 minutes • Cooking Time 50–55 minutes • Serves 4 • Per Serving 286 calories, 8g fat (1g saturated), 41g carbohydrates, 1,800mg sodium • Dairy Free • Easy

2 tablespoons olive oil
1 onion, finely sliced
2 garlic cloves, finely chopped
2 large leeks, sliced
5½ cups cherry tomatoes (about 1¾ pounds)
2 (15-ounce) cans lima beans, drained and rinsed
⅔ cup hot vegetable stock
½ tablespoon balsamic vinegar
salt and ground black pepper

1. Preheat the oven to 350°F. Heat the oil in a flameproof Dutch oven over medium heat. Add the onion and garlic and cook for 10 minutes, until golden brown and soft. Add the leeks and cook, covered, for 5 minutes.

2. Add the tomatoes, beans, and hot stock, and season well with salt and black pepper. Bring to a boil, cover, and bake in the oven for 35–40 minutes, until the sauce has thickened. Remove from the oven, stir in the vinegar, and spoon into warmed bowls.

Mushroom and Bean Stew

Preparation Time 15 minutes • Cooking Time 30 minutes • Serves 6 • Per Serving 280 calories, 10g fat (1g saturated), 34g carbohydrates, 1,300mg sodium • Dairy Free • Easy

3 tablespoons olive oil

1½ pounds cremini mushrooms, coarsely chopped

1 large onion, finely chopped

2 tablespoons all-purpose flour

2 tablespoons mild curry paste (see Cook's Tip)

⅔ cup dry white wine*

1 (14½-ounce) can diced tomatoes

2 tablespoons sun-dried tomato paste

4 cups canned mixed beans (such as kidney beans, pinto beans, and chickpeas), drained and rinsed

3 tablespoons mango chutney

3 tablespoons freshly chopped cilantro and mint

1. Heat the oil in a large saucepan over low heat. Sauté the mushrooms and onion until the onion is soft and browned. Stir in the flour and curry paste, and cook for 1–2 minutes.

2. Add the wine, tomatoes, sun-dried tomato paste, and beans, and bring to a boil. Then reduce the heat and simmer gently for 30 minutes or until most of the liquid has reduced. Stir in the chutney and herbs before serving.

This recipe is not suitable for children because it contains alcohol.

COOK'S TIP
Check the ingredients in the curry paste: some brands may not be suitable for vegetarians.

Eggplant and Lentil Curry

Preparation Time 10 minutes • Cooking Time 40–45 minutes • Serves 4 • Per Serving 335 calories, 15g fat (3g saturated), 39g carbohydrates, 200mg sodium • Easy

3 tablespoons olive oil

2 eggplants, cut into 1-inch chunks (see Cook's Tip)

1 onion, chopped

2 tablespoons mild curry paste (see Cook's Tip on page 83)

3 (14½-ounce) cans diced tomatoes

¾ cup hot vegetable stock

¾ cup red lentils, rinsed

3½ cups spinach leaves

½ cup freshly chopped cilantro

2 tablespoons fat-free Greek yogurt or soy yogurt

rice to serve

1. Heat 2 tablespoons of oil in a large saucepan over low heat and sauté the eggplant chunks until golden brown. Remove from the pan and put to one side.

2. Heat the remaining oil in the same pan and sauté the onion for 8–10 minutes, or until soft. Add the curry paste and sauté for another 2 minutes.

3. Add the tomatoes, hot stock, lentils, and eggplants to the pan. Bring to a boil. Then reduce the heat to a low simmer, cover halfway with a lid, and simmer for 25 minutes or according to the lentils' package directions.

4. At the end of cooking, stir the spinach, cilantro, and yogurt through the curry. Serve with rice.

COOK'S TIP

Choose eggplants that are firm, shiny, and blemish free, with a bright green stem.

Spicy Vegetable and Coconut Stir-Fry

Preparation Time 25 minutes • Cooking Time about 10 minutes • Serves 4 • Per Serving 200 calories, 11g fat (2g saturated), 21g carbohydrates, 1,400mg sodium • Dairy Free • Easy

2 tablespoons sesame oil
2 green chilies, seeded and finely chopped (see Cook's Tip on page 13)
1-inch piece fresh ginger, peeled and finely grated
2 garlic cloves, crushed
1 tablespoon Thai green curry paste (see Cook's Tip on page 83)
2 carrots, cut into fine sticks
8 baby corn, halved
2 cups snow peas, diagonally halved
2 large red bell peppers, seeded and finely sliced

2 small bok choy, quartered
4 scallions, finely chopped
1¼ cups coconut milk
2 tablespoons peanut satay sauce
2 tablespoons light soy sauce
1 teaspoon packed light brown sugar
¼ cup freshly chopped cilantro, plus extra sprigs to garnish
ground black pepper
roasted peanuts to garnish
rice or noodles to serve

1. Heat the oil in a wok or large nonstick skillet over medium heat. Add the chilies, ginger, and garlic, and stir-fry for 1 minute. Add the curry paste and cook for another 30 seconds.

2. Add the carrots, baby corn, snow peas, and bell peppers. Stir-fry over high heat for 3–4 minutes, and then add the bok choy and scallions. Cook, stirring, for another 1–2 minutes.

3. Pour in the coconut milk, satay sauce, soy sauce, and sugar, and season with black pepper. Bring to a boil and cook for 1–2 minutes. Then add the chopped cilantro. Garnish with the peanuts and cilantro sprigs and serve with rice or noodles.

Summer Vegetable Stir-Fry

Preparation Time 15 minutes • Cooking Time 7–8 minutes • Serves 4 • Per Serving 78 calories, 4g fat (1g saturated), 7g carbohydrates, trace sodium • Gluten Free • Dairy Free • Easy

12 baby carrots, scrubbed and trimmed
1 tablespoon sesame seeds
2 tablespoons sunflower oil
2 garlic cloves, roughly chopped
12 baby zucchini, halved lengthwise
1 large yellow bell pepper, seeded and cut into thick strips
12 thin asparagus spears, trimmed
8 cherry tomatoes, halved
2 tablespoons balsamic or sherry vinegar
1 teaspoon sesame oil
salt and ground black pepper

1. Blanch the carrots in lightly salted boiling water for 2 minutes. Then drain and pat dry.

2. Toast the sesame seeds in a hot, dry wok or large skillet over medium heat, stirring until they turn golden brown. Transfer to a plate.

3. Return the wok or skillet to the heat, add the sunflower oil, and heat until the oil is smoking. Add the garlic and stir-fry for 20 seconds. Add the carrots, zucchini, yellow bell pepper, and asparagus, and stir-fry over high heat for 1 minute.

4. Add the tomatoes and season to taste with salt and black pepper. Stir-fry for 3–4 minutes, until the vegetables are just tender. Add the vinegar and sesame oil, toss well, and sprinkle with the toasted sesame seeds. Serve immediately.

TRY SOMETHING DIFFERENT
Vary the vegetables, but always blanch the harder ones first. For a winter vegetable stir-fry, use cauliflower and broccoli florets, carrot sticks, 2–3 sliced scallions, and a little chopped fresh ginger.

Vegetable Moussaka

Preparation Time 45 minutes • Cooking Time about 1½ hours • Serves 6 • Per Serving 399 calories, 24g fat (11g saturated), 29g carbohydrates, 1,200mg sodium • Gluten Free • Easy

4 russet potatoes, peeled and cut lengthwise into ¼-inch slices
1 eggplant, sliced into rounds
1 large red onion, cut into wedges
2 red bell peppers, seeded and sliced
¼ cup olive oil
2 tablespoons freshly chopped thyme
2 tomatoes, thickly sliced
2 garlic cloves, sliced
1 cup canned tomato puree or tomato sauce
9 ounces soft goat cheese (see Cook's Tip on page 18)
1¼ cups plain yogurt
3 large eggs
¼ cup grated Parmesan cheese
salt and ground black pepper
green salad to serve

1. Preheat the oven to 450°F. Parboil the potatoes in a saucepan of lightly salted water for 5 minutes. Drain and put into a large roasting pan with the eggplant, onion, and bell peppers. Drizzle with the oil, add the thyme, toss, and season with salt and black pepper. Roast for 30 minutes, stirring occasionally.

2. Add the tomatoes and garlic, roast for 15 minutes, and then take it out of the oven. Reduce the oven temperature to 400°F.

3. Put half the vegetables into a 1½-quart ovenproof dish. Spoon half the canned tomato puree or sauce over them and spread the goat cheese on top. Repeat with the rest of the vegetables and canned tomato puree or sauce. Mix together the yogurt, eggs, and Parmesan. Season and then pour over the top. Bake in the oven for 45 minutes or until heated through. Serve with a green salad.

TRY SOMETHING DIFFERENT
Use sliced sweet potatoes or butternut squash, seeded and cut into chunks, instead of the potatoes.

Eggplant Parmesan

Preparation Time 10 minutes • Cooking Time 25 minutes • Serves 4 • Per Serving 432 calories, 28g fat (11g saturated), 25g carbohydrates, 2,400mg sodium • Gluten Free • Easy

2 large eggplants, thinly sliced lengthwise

2 tablespoons olive oil, plus extra to brush

3 fat garlic cloves, sliced

2 (8-ounce) jars marinara sauce

4 roasted red bell peppers, coarsely chopped

½ cup freshly chopped basil (see Cook's Tip)

1 cup shredded Taleggio, fontina, or mozzarella cheese (see Cook's Tip on page 18)

½ cup coarsely grated Parmesan cheese

salt and ground black pepper

green salad to serve

1. Preheat the broiler until hot. Put the eggplants on a greased baking sheet, brush with oil, sprinkle with garlic, and season with salt and black pepper. Broil for 5–6 minutes, until golden brown.

2. Reduce the heat to 400°F. Spread a little marinara sauce over the bottom of an oiled ovenproof dish. Then cover with a layer of eggplant and roasted peppers, packing the layers together as tightly as you can. Sprinkle a little basil and some of each cheese over the top. Repeat the layers, finishing with a layer of cheese. Season with black pepper. Cook in the oven for 20 minutes or until golden brown. Serve hot with a green salad.

COOK'S TIP

Choose bags or bunches of fresh basil. The larger leaves have a stronger, more peppery flavor than those of the plants sold in flowerpots.

SIDE
DISHES

Asparagus and Snow Peas with Lemon Sauce

Preparation Time 5–10 minutes • Cooking Time 10 minutes • Serves 4 • Per Serving 114 calories, 6g fat (1g saturated), 10g carbohydrates, trace sodium • Dairy Free • Easy

8 ounces asparagus spears, trimmed and cut diagonally into three pieces
1 tablespoon sesame seeds
1 tablespoon vegetable oil
1 teaspoon sesame oil
4 cups snow peas
1 garlic clove, crushed
2 tablespoons dry sherry*
1 tablespoon superfine sugar
2 teaspoons light soy sauce
grated zest and juice of 1 lemon, plus extra zest to garnish
1 teaspoon cornstarch
⅓ cup water
salt
strips of lemon zest to garnish

1. Cook the asparagus in a saucepan of lightly salted boiling water for about 5 minutes until just tender. Drain well.

2. Meanwhile, toast the sesame seeds in a hot wok or large skillet until golden brown. Transfer to a plate and set aside.

3. Return the wok or skillet to the heat and add the vegetable and sesame oils. Add the snow peas, garlic, and asparagus, and stir-fry for 2 minutes.

4. Put the sherry, sugar, soy sauce, lemon zest and juice, cornstarch, and the water into a bowl and mix.

5. Pour the mixture into the wok or skillet and cook, stirring, until the sauce thickens and coats the vegetables. Sprinkle with toasted sesame seeds, garnish with lemon zest, and serve immediately.

* This recipe is not suitable for children because it contains alcohol.

Baked Tomatoes and Fennel

Preparation Time 10 minutes • Cooking Time 1¼ hours • Serves 6 • Per Serving 127 calories, 9g fat (1g saturated), 7g carbohydrates, 100mg sodium • Gluten Free • Dairy Free • Easy

2 pounds fennel, trimmed and cut into quarters
⅓ cup white wine*
5 fresh thyme sprigs
⅓ cup olive oil
8 ripe beefsteak or 16 plum tomatoes (about 2 pounds)

1. Preheat the oven to 400°F. Put the fennel into a roasting pan and pour the white wine over it. Snip the thyme sprigs over the fennel, drizzle with the oil, and roast for 45 minutes.

2. Halve the tomatoes, add to the roasting pan, and continue to roast for 30 minutes or until tender, basting with the juices halfway through.

* This recipe is not suitable for children because it contains alcohol.

COOK'S TIP
This is an ideal accompaniment to a vegetarian frittata.

Baked Potatoes with Mustard Seeds

Preparation Time 15–20 minutes • Cooking Time 1¼ hours • Serves 6 • Per Serving 315 calories, 17g fat (9g saturated), 38g carbohydrates, 1,000mg sodium • Gluten Free • Easy

6 large russet potatoes (about 3 pounds), scrubbed
2 tablespoons sunflower oil
1 tablespoon coarse sea salt
4–5 large garlic cloves, unpeeled
4 tablespoons butter
⅓ cup crème fraîche or sour cream
2 tablespoons mustard seeds, toasted and lightly crushed
salt and ground black pepper
fresh oregano sprigs to garnish

1. Preheat the oven to 400°F. Prick the potato skins all over with a fork, rub with oil, and sprinkle with the sea salt. Bake in the oven for 1 hour. About 20 minutes before the end of the cooking time, put the garlic cloves in a small roasting pan and cook for 20 minutes.

2. Squeeze the potatoes gently to check they are well cooked. Then remove the potatoes and garlic from the oven and let cool slightly. When cool enough to handle, slice the tops off the potatoes and scoop the flesh into a warm bowl. Squeeze the garlic out of its skin and add it to the potato flesh with the butter, crème fraîche or sour cream, and mustard seeds. Season to taste with salt and black pepper, and mash well. Return the potato mixture to the hollowed skins.

3. Put the filled potatoes on a baking sheet and return to the oven for 15 minutes or until golden brown. Garnish with oregano sprigs and serve hot.

FREEZING TIP

To freeze Complete the recipe to the end of step 2. Then cool, wrap, and freeze for up to one month.
To use Thaw overnight at cool room temperature. Cook at 400°F for 20–25 minutes or until piping hot in the center.

Braised Endives

Preparation Time 5 minutes • Cooking Time about 1 hour • Serves 6 • Per Serving 80 calories, 7g fat (5g saturated), 3g carbohydrates, 100mg sodium • Gluten Free • Easy

4 tablespoons butter, softened
6 heads endives, trimmed
½ cup white wine*
salt and ground black pepper
freshly snipped chives to serve

1. Preheat the oven to 375°F. Grease a 1½-quart ovenproof dish with 1 tablespoon butter and lay the endives in the dish.

2. Season to taste, add the wine, and dot the remaining butter over the top. Cover with aluminum foil and cook in the oven for 1 hour or until soft. Sprinkle with chives to serve.

* This recipe is not suitable for children because it contains alcohol.

Braised Red Cabbage

Preparation Time 15 minutes • Cooking Time about 50 minutes • Serves 6 • Per Serving 63 calories, 1g fat (0g saturated), 12g carbohydrates, 900mg sodium • Gluten Free • Dairy Free • Easy

1 tablespoon olive oil
1 red onion, halved and sliced
2 garlic cloves, crushed
1 large red cabbage (about 2¼ pounds), shredded
2 tablespoons packed light brown sugar
2 tablespoons red wine vinegar
8 juniper berries
¼ teaspoon ground allspice
1¼ cups vegetable stock
2 pears, cored and sliced
salt and ground black pepper
fresh thyme sprigs to garnish

1. Heat the oil in a large saucepan, add the onion, and sauté for 5 minutes. Add the remaining ingredients, except the pears, and season with salt and black pepper. Bring to a boil, and then reduce the heat, cover, and simmer for 30 minutes.

2. Add the pears and cook for another 15 minutes or until nearly all the liquid has evaporated and the cabbage is tender. Serve hot, garnished with thyme.

GET AHEAD

To prepare ahead *Braised red cabbage improves if made a day ahead. Complete the recipe to the end of step 1, cover, and chill.*
To use *Reheat the cabbage gently, add the pears, and complete the recipe.*

Charred Zucchini

Preparation Time 5 minutes • Cooking Time 10 minutes • Serves 4 • Per Serving 36 calories,
2g fat (trace saturated), 2g carbohydrates, trace sodium • Gluten Free • Dairy Free • Easy

4 zucchini, halved lengthwise
olive oil to brush
coarse sea salt to sprinkle

1. Preheat the barbecue or a ridged griddle pan. Score a crisscross pattern on the fleshy side of the zucchini. Brush lightly with oil and sprinkle with sea salt.

2. Cook the zucchini on the barbecue or griddle pan for 10 minutes or until just tender, turning occasionally.

TRY SOMETHING DIFFERENT

Mix the olive oil with a good pinch of dried red pepper flakes and a small handful of freshly chopped rosemary leaves.

Use a mixture of yellow and green zucchini, if desired.

Zucchini with Sesame Seeds

Preparation Time 5 minutes • Cooking Time 12 minutes • Serves 6 • Per Serving 107 calories,
9g fat (1g saturated), 3g carbohydrates, 400mg sodium • Gluten Free • Dairy Free • Easy

2 tablespoons sesame seeds
2 tablespoons vegetable oil
4 garlic cloves, crushed
4 zucchini (about 2 pounds), thinly
   sliced
1 scallion, thickly sliced
½ teaspoon salt
1 tablespoon sesame oil
ground black pepper
banana leaves to serve (optional,
   see Cook's Tip)

1. Toast the sesame seeds in a hot wok or large skillet until golden brown. Transfer to a plate.

2. Heat the vegetable oil in the wok or skillet. Add the garlic and sauté for 2 minutes.

3. Add the zucchini and stir-fry for 7–8 minutes. Stir in the scallion, salt, and sesame oil, and season to taste with black pepper. Cook for another minute, and then add the toasted sesame seeds. Stir once and serve hot or cold on a bed of banana leaves, if desired.

COOK'S TIP
Banana leaves are sometimes used instead of plates in Southeast Asia. They make an unusual presentation and are available at some Asian food stores.

Roasted Butternut Squash

Preparation Time 15 minutes • Cooking Time 40 minutes • Serves 4 • Per Serving 165 calories, 12g fat (5g saturated), 11g carbohydrates, 100mg sodium • Gluten Free • Easy

- **2 butternut squash**
- **2 tablespoons olive oil**
- **2 tablespoons butter**
- **2 tablespoons freshly chopped thyme leaves**
- **1 red chili, seeded and finely chopped (see Cook's Tip on page 13)**
- **salt and ground black pepper**

1. Preheat the oven to 425°F. Cut the squash in half lengthwise and scoop out the seeds. Cut in half again, and then put into a roasting pan. Drizzle with the oil, season with salt and black pepper, and roast for 40 minutes.

2. Meanwhile, put the butter into a bowl with the thyme and chili. Mix together well. Add a little to each slice of cooked butternut squash and serve.

TRY SOMETHING DIFFERENT
Use crushed garlic instead of red chili.

Roasted Mediterranean Vegetables

Preparation Time 10 minutes • Cooking Time 35–40 minutes • Serves 4 • Per Serving 252 calories, 18g fat (3g saturated), 19g carbohydrates, 400mg sodium • Gluten Free • Dairy Free • Easy

4 plum tomatoes, halved
2 onions, quartered
4 red bell peppers, seeded and cut into strips
2 zucchini, cut into thick slices
4 garlic cloves, unpeeled
⅓ cup olive oil
1 tablespoon freshly chopped thyme leaves
sea salt flakes and ground black pepper

1. Preheat the oven to 425°F. Put the tomatoes into a large roasting pan with the onions, bell peppers, zucchini, and garlic. Drizzle with the oil and sprinkle with thyme, sea salt flakes, and black pepper.

2. Roast, turning occasionally, for 35–40 minutes, until tender.

COOK'S TIP

To make a nutritionally complete meal, sprinkle with toasted sesame seeds and serve with hummus (see page 67).

TRY SOMETHING DIFFERENT

Use fresh oregano instead of thyme.

Roasted Rosemary Potatoes

Preparation Time 10 minutes • Cooking Time 20–25 minutes • Serves 8 • Per Serving 102 calories, 4g fat (1g saturated), 15g carbohydrates, trace sodium • Gluten Free • Dairy Free • Easy

1¾ pounds new potatoes, scrubbed
   (see Cook's Tip)
3 tablespoons olive oil
8 fresh rosemary stalks, each
   about 7 inches long
salt and ground black pepper

1. Preheat the barbecue or broiler. Cook the potatoes, unpeeled, in lightly salted boiling water for 10 minutes or until nearly tender. Drain, cool a little, and then toss in the oil. Season well.

2. Strip most of the leaves from the rosemary stalks, leaving a few at the tip; set the stripped leaves to one side.

3. Thread the potatoes onto the rosemary stems, place on the hot barbecue or under the broiler, and sprinkle with the leaves. Cook for 10–15 minutes, turning from time to time, until tender and lightly charred.

COOK'S TIP

Skewering the potatoes helps them to cook quicker and makes them easier to handle on a barbecue. Using rosemary stems adds a wonderful flavor.

Sage-Roasted Parsnips, Apples, and Prunes

Preparation Time 20 minutes • Cooking Time 45–55 minutes • Serves 8 • Per Serving 313 calories, 16g fat (5g saturated), 40g carbohydrates, 200mg sodium • Gluten Free • Easy

⅓ – ½ cup olive oil

4 pounds parsnips, peeled, quartered, and cored

6 Pippin, Rome, or Jonagold apples, peeled, cored, and quartered

16 prunes, pitted

4 tablespoons butter

1–2 tablespoons freshly chopped sage leaves

1–2 tablespoons honey (optional)

salt and ground black pepper

1. Heat 3–4 tablespoons of oil in a large flameproof roasting pan. Add the parsnips in batches, and sauté over medium heat until a rich golden brown all over. Remove from the pan and set aside. Add 3–4 tablespoons of oil to the same pan. Sauté the apples until golden brown. Remove from the pan and set aside.

2. Preheat the oven to 400°F. Put the parsnips back into the pan, season with salt and black pepper, and roast for 15 minutes.

3. Add the apples and continue roasting for 10 minutes. Add the prunes to the pan and roast for another 5 minutes. At the end of this time, test the apples; if they're still firm, roast everything for another 5–10 minutes, until the apples are soft and fluffy.

4. Put the pan on the stove over low heat. Add the butter and sage, drizzle with honey, if desired, and spoon into a hot serving dish.

GET AHEAD

To prepare ahead *Sauté the parsnips and apples. Then cool, cover, and chill for up to one day.* **To use** *Complete the recipe.*

Lemon and Orange Carrots

Preparation Time 10 minutes • Cooking Time 10–15 minutes • Serves 8 • Per Serving 127 calories,
6g fat (3g saturated), 17g carbohydrates, 200mg sodium • Gluten Free • Easy

**2 pounds carrots, cut into long
    sticks**
⅔ cup orange juice
juice of 2 lemons
⅔ cup dry white wine*
4 tablespoons butter
**3 tablespoons packed light
    brown sugar**
**¼ cup freshly chopped cilantro
    to garnish**

1. Put the carrots, orange and lemon juices, wine, butter, and sugar into a saucepan. Cover and bring to a boil.

2. Remove the lid and cook for about 10 minutes until almost all the liquid has evaporated. Serve sprinkled with the cilantro.

* This recipe is not suitable for children because it contains alcohol.

FREEZING TIP
To freeze *Cook the carrots for only 5 minutes, and then cool and freeze with the remaining liquid.*
To use *Thaw for 5 hours, and then reheat in a saucepan for 5–6 minutes, or cook on full power in a 900W microwave for 7–8 minutes.*

Sweet Roasted Fennel

Preparation Time 10 minutes • Cooking Time about 1 hour • Serves 4 • Per Serving 192 calories, 19g fat (8g saturated), 4g carbohydrates, 200mg sodium • Gluten Free • Easy

3 fennel bulbs (about 1½ pounds)
3 tablespoons olive oil
4 tablespoons butter, melted
1 lemon, halved
1 teaspoon superfine sugar
2 large fresh thyme sprigs
salt and ground black pepper

1. Preheat the oven to 400°F. Trim and quarter the fennel and put into a large roasting pan.

2. Drizzle the fennel with the oil and melted butter, and squeeze the lemon juice over the top. Add the lemon halves to the roasting pan. Sprinkle with sugar and season generously with salt and black pepper. Add the thyme and cover with a damp piece of nonstick parchment paper.

3. Roast for 30 minutes. Then remove the parchment paper and cook for another 20–30 minutes until lightly charred and tender.

Spinach with Tomatoes

Preparation Time 10 minutes • Cooking Time 15 minutes • Serves 4 • Per Serving 85 calories,
7g fat (5g saturated), 3g carbohydrates, 300mg sodium • Gluten Free • Easy

4 tablespoons butter
2 garlic cloves, crushed
3 cups baby plum tomatoes, halved
1½ (6-ounce) bags baby spinach
**a large pinch of freshly grated
  nutmeg**
salt and ground black pepper

1. Heat half the butter in a
saucepan, add the garlic, and cook
until just soft. Add the tomatoes and
cook for 4–5 minutes, until just
beginning to soften.

2. Put the spinach and a little water
into a clean saucepan, cover, and
cook for 2–3 minutes, until just
wilted. Drain well, coarsely chop,
and stir into the tomatoes.

3. Add the remaining butter and
heat through gently. Season well
with salt and black pepper, stir in
the nutmeg, and serve.

Green Beans and Slivered Almonds

Preparation Time 5 minutes • Cooking Time 5–7 minutes • Serves 4 • Per Serving 57 calories, 5g fat (trace saturated), 2g carbohydrates, 0mg sodium • Gluten Free • Dairy Free • Easy

8 ounces green beans, trimmed
1 teaspoon olive oil
¼ cup slivered almonds
½ lemon

1. Bring a large saucepan of water to a boil. Add the green beans and cook for 4–5 minutes. Drain.

2. Meanwhile, heat the oil in a large skillet. Add the almonds and cook for 1–2 minutes, until golden brown. Turn off the heat, add the drained beans to the pan, and toss. Squeeze a little lemon juice over the green beans just before serving.

TRY SOMETHING DIFFERENT

Use basil-infused oil and increase the amount of oil to 2 tablespoons.

Use pine nuts instead of almonds, drizzle with balsamic vinegar, and sprinkle with basil leaves to serve.

Stir-Fried Beans with Cherry Tomatoes

Preparation Time 10 minutes • Cooking Time about 8 minutes • Serves 4 • Per Serving 30 calories, 2g fat (trace saturated), 3g carbohydrates, trace sodium • Gluten Free • Dairy Free • Easy

12 ounces green beans, trimmed
2 teaspoons olive oil
1 large garlic clove, crushed
1 cup cherry or baby plum
**   tomatoes, halved**
2 tablespoons freshly chopped
**   Italian parsley**
salt and ground black pepper

1. Cook the beans in lightly salted boiling water for 4–5 minutes, and then drain well.

2. Heat the oil in a wok or large skillet over high heat. Stir-fry the beans with the garlic and tomatoes for 2–3 minutes, until the beans are tender and the tomatoes are just beginning to soften without losing their shape. Season well with salt and black pepper, stir in the parsley, and serve.

Stir-Fried Green Vegetables

Preparation Time 5 minutes • Cooking Time 3–4 minutes • Serves 6 • Per Serving 100 calories, 8g fat (3g saturated), 5g carbohydrates, 100mg sodium • Gluten Free • Easy

2 tablespoons vegetable oil
2 small zucchini, thinly sliced
3 cups snow peas
2 tablespoons butter
1¾ cups frozen peas, thawed
salt and ground black pepper

1. Heat the oil in a wok or large skillet, add the zucchini, and stir-fry for 1–2 minutes.

2. Add the snow peas and cook for 1 minute. Add the butter and the thawed peas and cook for 1 minute. Season to taste with salt and black pepper and serve immediately.

TRY SOMETHING DIFFERENT
Try other vegetables, such as thinly sliced leeks, scallions, or bok choy.

EGG AND
CHEESE DISHES

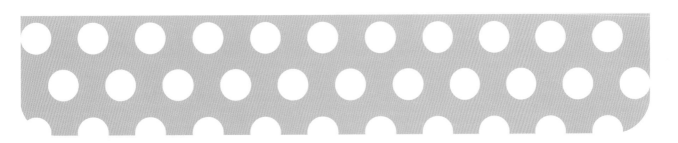

Poached Eggs with Mushrooms

Preparation Time 15 minutes • Cooking Time 20 minutes • Serves 4 • Per Serving 276 calories, 23g fat (9g saturated), 1g carbohydrates, 700mg sodium • Gluten Free • Easy

8 medium flat or portabello mushrooms
3 tablespoons butter
8 large eggs
1 (6-ounce) bag baby spinach leaves
4 teaspoons fresh pesto (see Cook's Tip on page 14)

1. Preheat the oven to 400°F. Arrange the mushrooms in a single layer in a small roasting pan and dot with the butter. Roast for 15 minutes or until golden brown and soft.

2. Meanwhile, bring a wide, shallow saucepan of water to a boil. When the mushrooms are cooked halfway and the water is boiling furiously, break the eggs into the pan of boiling water, spaced well apart, and then remove the pan from the heat. The eggs will take about 6 minutes to poach.

3. When the mushrooms are tender, put them onto a warmed plate, cover, and return to the turned-off oven to keep warm.

4. Put the roasting pan over medium heat on the stove and add the spinach. Cook, stirring, for about 30 seconds or until the spinach has just started to wilt.

5. The eggs should be set by now, so divide the mushrooms among four warmed plates and top with a little spinach, a poached egg, and a teaspoon of pesto.

TRY SOMETHING DIFFERENT
For a more substantial meal, serve on rye or pumpernickel bread.

Classic French Omelet

Preparation Time 5 minutes • Cooking Time 5 minutes • Serves 1 • Per Serving 449 calories,
40g fat (19g saturated), 1g carbohydrates, 1,000mg sodium • Gluten Free • Easy

2–3 large eggs
1 tablespoon milk or water
2 tablespoons unsalted butter
salt and ground black pepper
sliced or roasted tomatoes and
**   freshly chopped Italian parsley**
**   to serve**

1. Whisk the eggs in a bowl, just enough to break them down; overbeating will ruin the texture of the omelet. Season with salt and black pepper and add the milk or water.

2. Heat the butter in a 7-inch omelet pan or nonstick skillet until it is foaming but not brown. Add the eggs and stir gently with a fork or wooden spatula, drawing the mixture from the sides to the center as it sets and letting the liquid egg in the center run to the sides. When set, stop stirring and cook for 30 seconds or until the omelet is golden brown underneath and still creamy on top: don't overcook. If you are making a filled omelet (see Try Something Different), add the filling at this point.

3. Tilt the pan away from you slightly and use a spatula to fold over one-third of the omelet to the center. Then fold over the opposite third. Slide the omelet out onto a warmed plate, letting it flip over so that the folded sides are underneath. Serve immediately with tomatoes sprinkled with parsley.

TRY SOMETHING DIFFERENT
Blend 1 ounce mild goat cheese (see Cook's Tip on page 18) with 1 tablespoon crème fraîche; put in the center of the omelet before folding.

good!

Sweet Potato and Goat Cheese Frittata

Preparation Time 15 minutes • Cooking Time 1 hour 50 minutes • Serves 8 • 316 calories, 22g fat (11g saturated), 20g carbohydrates, 700mg sodium • Easy

- 2 large sweet potatoes, peeled and thinly sliced
- 3 tablespoons olive oil
- 3 bell peppers (mixed red and yellow), seeded and coarsely chopped
- 1 fennel bulb, thinly sliced
- 3 garlic cloves, crushed
- 1 small onion, thinly sliced
- 3 large eggs
- 1¼ cups light cream
- 4 ounces each fresh soft goat cheese and Taleggio cheese, chopped (see Cook's Tip on page 18)
- 3 cups young spinach or fresh basil
- salt and ground black pepper

1. Preheat the oven to 425°F. Put the potatoes into a large roasting pan, season with salt and black pepper, and drizzle with half the oil. Toss well. Put the bell peppers, fennel, garlic, and onion into a second roasting pan. Season, drizzle with the remaining oil, and toss well. Put both pans into the oven and roast for 30–35 minutes, until the vegetables are tender.

2. Whisk together the eggs, cream, and cheese, and season with plenty of coarsely ground black pepper.

3. Line the bottom and sides of an 8-inch round, 3-inch deep cake pan with nonstick parchment paper.

4. Reduce the oven temperature to 325°F. Layer the roasted vegetables in the cake pan with the spinach or basil, adding a little egg mix as you work. Pour in any remaining egg mixture and cook the tortilla in the center of the oven for about 1 hour 15 minutes or until the egg is set and the top golden brown. Serve warm or cold.

Zucchini and Parmesan Frittata

Preparation Time 10 minutes • Cooking Time 15–20 minutes • Serves 4 • Per Serving 229 calories, 19g fat (9g saturated), 2g carbohydrates, 600mg sodium • Gluten Free • Easy

3 tablespoons butter
1 small onion, finely chopped
1 zucchini, finely sliced
6 large eggs, beaten
¼ cup freshly grated Parmesan cheese, plus shavings to garnish (see Cook's Tip on page 18)
salt and ground black pepper
green salad to serve

1. Melt 2 tablespoons butter in a 7-inch nonstick skillet and cook the onion for about 10 minutes or until softened. Add the zucchini and sauté gently for 5 minutes or until it begins to soften.

2. Beat the eggs in a bowl and season with salt and black pepper.

3. Add the remaining butter to the pan and heat. Then pour in the eggs. Cook for 2–3 minutes, until golden brown underneath and cooked around the edges. Meanwhile, preheat the broiler to medium.

4. Sprinkle the grated cheese over the frittata and broil for 1–2 minutes, until just set. Sprinkle with Parmesan shavings, cut the frittata into quarters, and serve with a green salad.

TRY SOMETHING DIFFERENT
Cherry Tomato and Arugula Frittata
Replace the zucchini with 12 ripe cherry tomatoes, sautéing them for only 1 minute, or until they begin to soften. Immediately after pouring in the eggs, sprinkle 1 cup arugula over the surface. Continue cooking as in step 3.

Mixed Mushroom Frittata

Preparation Time 15 minutes • Cooking Time 15–20 minutes • Serves 4 • 148 calories, 12g fat (3g saturated), 0g carbohydrates, 300mg sodium • Dairy Free • Gluten Free

1 tablespoon olive oil

12 ounces mixed mushrooms, sliced

2 tablespoons freshly chopped thyme

grated zest and juice of ½ lemon

2 cups spinach, chopped

6 large eggs, beaten

salt and ground black pepper

whole-wheat bread (optional) and a crisp green salad to serve

1. Heat the oil in a large, deep skillet over medium heat. Add the mushrooms and thyme, and stir-fry for 4–5 minutes, until the mixture starts to soften and brown. Stir in the lemon zest and juice, and then simmer for another minute. Reduce the heat.

2. Preheat the broiler. Add the spinach to the beaten eggs, season with salt and black pepper, and pour into the pan. Cook on the stove for 7–8 minutes, until the sides and bottoms are firm but the center is still a little soft.

3. Transfer to the broiler and cook for 4–5 minutes, until just set. Cut into wedges and serve with chunks of bread, if desired, and a salad.

Spinach and Goat Cheese Frittata

Preparation Time 10 minutes • Cooking Time 12 minutes • Serves 4 • Per Serving 281 calories, 21g fat (9g saturated), 3g carbohydrates, 900mg sodium • Gluten Free • Easy

6–8 baby leeks, trimmed and chopped
4 scallions, chopped
4 cups baby spinach
6 extra-large eggs
¼ cup milk
freshly grated nutmeg
4 ounces soft goat cheese, chopped (see Cook's Tip on page 18)
1 tablespoon olive oil
salt and ground black pepper
mixed salad greens to serve

1. Preheat the broiler to high. Blanch the leeks in a saucepan of lightly salted boiling water for 2 minutes. Add the scallions and spinach just before the end of the cooking time. Drain, rinse in cold water, and dry on paper towels.

2. Whisk together the eggs, milk, and nutmeg. Season with salt and black pepper. Stir the goat cheese into the egg mixture with the leeks, spinach, and scallions.

3. Heat the oil in a nonstick skillet. Pour in the frittata mixture and sauté gently for 4–5 minutes. Then finish under the hot broiler for 4–5 minutes, until the top is golden brown and just firm. Serve with mixed salad.

TRY SOMETHING DIFFERENT
Use a different cheese, such as Stilton.

Twice-Baked Soufflés

Preparation Time 20 minutes, plus cooling • Cooking Time 1¼ hours • Serves 8 •
Per Serving 377 calories, 34g fat (20g saturated), 7g carbohydrates, 600mg sodium • A Little Effort

4 tablespoons butter, plus extra to grease
¼ cup ground almonds (almond meal), lightly toasted
2 cups cauliflower florets
⅔ cup milk
¼ cup all-purpose flour
¾ cup finely shredded cheddar cheese (see Cook's Tip on page 18)
¾ cup finely shredded Swiss cheese
3 extra-large eggs, separated
1¼ cups heavy cream
1 tablespoon whole-grain mustard
salt and ground black pepper
arugula and cherry tomatoes drizzled with olive oil and balsamic vinegar to serve

1. Preheat the oven to 350°F. Grease eight ⅔-cup ramekins and line the bottom with parchment paper. Dust with the ground almonds.

2. Cook the cauliflower in lightly salted boiling water until tender. Drain, plunge into ice water, and drain again. Blend with the milk until smooth.

3. Melt the butter in a saucepan, add the flour, and mix to a smooth paste. Stir in the cauliflower puree and bring to a boil. Cool a little. Beat in the cheeses and egg yolks and season.

4. Whisk the egg whites to a soft peak and fold in. Spoon the mixture into the ramekins, put into a roasting pan, and fill the pan halfway with hot water. Bake for 20–25 minutes, until firm to the touch. Remove from the pan and cool completely. Run a knife around the edge of the soufflés and turn out onto a baking sheet.

5. Preheat the oven to 400°F. Bring the cream to a boil in a wide saucepan. Simmer until reduced by one-third. Add the mustard and season. Spoon a little cream over the soufflés and bake for 15–20 minutes, until golden brown. Serve with dressed arugula and cherry tomatoes.

FREEZING TIP

To freeze *Prepare the recipe to the first baking, turn out onto a baking sheet, and cool. Then wrap separately, label, and freeze for up to one month.*
To use *Complete the recipe. Cook the soufflés from frozen at 400°F for 25–30 minutes, until golden.*

Grilled Sweet Potatoes with Feta and Olives

Preparation Time 15 minutes • Cooking Time 15–20 minutes • Serves 4 • Per Serving 324 calories, 23g fat (9g saturated), 21g carbohydrates, 2,500mg sodium • Gluten Free • Easy

1 large sweet potato
¼ cup olive oil, plus extra to brush
7 ounces feta cheese (see Cook's Tip on page 18)
2 teaspoons dried Herbes de Provence (see Cook's Tip)
¼ cup ripe black olives, pitted and chopped
1 garlic clove, crushed
salt and ground black pepper
fresh Italian parsley sprigs to garnish

1. Preheat the barbecue or ridged griddle pan. Peel the sweet potato and cut lengthwise into eight wedges. Put them into a saucepan of boiling water and bring back to a boil. Then simmer for 3 minutes. Drain and refresh in cold water. Drain, dry well on paper towels, and brush lightly with oil. Season with salt and black pepper, and then grill for 10–15 minutes, until well browned and cooked through.

2. Meanwhile, mash together the cheese, herbs, olives, garlic, and ¼ cup of oil. Serve the sweet potato with the feta cheese mixture, garnished with Italian parsley.

COOK'S TIP
Herbes de Provence, an aromatic dried mixture made up of rosemary, thyme, basil, bay, and savory, is a wonderful complement to grilled food.

Pasta and Vegetable Gratin

Preparation Time 15 minutes • Cooking Time 15 minutes • Serves 4 • Per Serving 471 calories,
13g fat (7g saturated), 67g carbohydrates, 800mg sodium • Easy

8 ounces macaroni

1 cauliflower, cut into florets

2 leeks, trimmed and finely
   chopped

¾ cup frozen peas

¼ cup whole-wheat bread crumbs

crusty bread to serve

FOR THE CHEESE SAUCE

1 tablespoon butter

2 tablespoons all-purpose flour

¾ cup skim milk

¾ cup grated Parmesan cheese
   (see Cook's Tip on page 18)

2 teaspoons Dijon mustard

salt and ground black pepper

1. Cook the macaroni in a large saucepan of boiling water according to the package directions, adding the cauliflower and leeks for the last 4 minutes and the peas for the last 2 minutes.

2. Meanwhile, make the cheese sauce (also see Cook's Tip). Melt the butter in a saucepan and add the flour. Cook for 1–2 minutes, and then remove from heat and gradually stir in the milk. Bring to a boil slowly, stirring until the sauce thickens. Stir in ½ cup Parmesan and the mustard. Season with salt and black pepper.

3. Preheat the broiler to medium. Drain the pasta and vegetables and put back into the pan. Add the cheese sauce and mix well. Spoon into a large shallow 1-quart ovenproof dish. Sprinkle the remaining Parmesan and the bread crumbs over the top. Broil for 5 minutes or until golden brown and crisp. Serve hot with bread.

COOK'S TIP
Microwave Cheese Sauce
Put the butter, flour, and milk into a large microwave-proof bowl and whisk together. Cook in a 900W microwave oven on full power for 4 minutes, whisking every minute until the sauce has thickened. Stir in the cheese until it melts. Stir in the mustard and season to taste.

Cheese Fondue Tarts

Preparation Time 20 minutes, plus chilling • Cooking Time 25 minutes • Serves 6 •
Per Serving 337 calories, 22g fat (3g saturated), 28g carbohydrates, 600mg sodium • Easy

butter to grease
flour to dust
2 sheets ready-to-bake puff pastry,
   thawed if frozen
1¾ cups each shredded Jarlsberg
   and Gouda cheese (see Cook's
   Tip on page 18)
1 garlic clove, crushed

⅔ cup light cream
juice of 1 small lemon
½ teaspoon paprika
2 teaspoons cornstarch
¼ cup vodka*
2 tablespoons freshly chopped dill,
   plus extra to garnish

1. Preheat the oven to 425°F and grease a 12-cup muffin pan. On a lightly floured surface, roll out the pastry to ⅛ inch thick. Cut out twelve 4-inch circles and put into the pan. Prick the bottoms and chill for 10 minutes. Line with parchment paper and fill with pie weights or dried beans. Bake for 15–20 minutes, remove the paper and weights, and bake for another 5 minutes or until golden brown.

2. Meanwhile, put the cheese, garlic, cream, lemon juice, and paprika into a saucepan. Heat and stir to make a smooth sauce. Mix the cornstarch with the vodka, add to the pan, and cook for 1–2 minutes. Stir in the dill.

3. Spoon the mixture into the pastry shells, sprinkle with dill, and serve warm.

* This recipe is not suitable for children because it contains alcohol.

Roasted Stuffed Peppers

Preparation Time 20 minutes • Cooking Time 50 minutes • Serves 8 • Per Serving 189 calories, 14g fat (6g saturated), 11g carbohydrates, 900mg sodium • Easy

3 tablespoons butter
4 Romano peppers, halved with stems on, and seeded
3 tablespoons olive oil
12 ounces cremini mushrooms, coarsely chopped
¼ cup freshly chopped chives
4 ounces feta cheese (see Cook's Tip on page 18)
1 cup fresh white bread crumbs
¼ cup freshly grated Parmesan cheese
salt and ground black pepper

1. Preheat the oven to 350°F. Use a little of the butter to grease a shallow ovenproof dish and put the Romano peppers in it side by side, cut side up, ready to be filled.

2. Heat the remaining butter and 1 tablespoon oil in a saucepan. Add the mushrooms and sauté until they're golden brown and there is no excess liquid left in the pan. Stir in the chives, and then spoon the mixture into the Romano pepper halves.

3. Crumble the feta over the mushrooms. Mix the bread crumbs and Parmesan in a bowl. Then sprinkle the mixture over the Romano peppers.

4. Season with salt and black pepper, and drizzle with the remaining oil. Roast in the oven for 45 minutes or until golden brown and tender. Serve warm.

GET AHEAD
To prepare ahead Up to one day in advance, complete the recipe to the end of step 4. Cover and chill.
To use Reheat under the broiler for 5 minutes.

LEGUMES AND GRAINS

Lentil Chili

Preparation Time 10 minutes • Cooking Time 30 minutes • Serves 6 • Per Serving 195 calories,
2g fat (trace saturated), 32g carbohydrates, 100mg sodium • Gluten Free • Easy

oil-water spray (see Cook's Tip)
2 red onions, chopped
1½ teaspoons each ground coriander and ground cumin
½ teaspoon ground paprika
2 garlic cloves, crushed
2 sun-dried tomatoes, chopped
¼ teaspoon crushed red pepper flakes
½ cup red wine*

1¼ cups hot vegetable stock
2 (15½-ounce) cans brown or green lentils, drained and rinsed, or 4 cups cooked brown or green lentils
2 (14½-ounce) cans diced tomatoes
sugar to taste
salt and ground black pepper
plain low-fat yogurt or soy yogurt and rice to serve

1. Spray a saucepan with the oil-water spray and cook the onions for 5 minutes or until softened. Add the coriander, cumin, and paprika. Add the garlic, sun-dried tomatoes, red pepper flakes, wine, and hot stock to the pan. Cover and simmer for 5–7 minutes. Uncover and simmer until the onions are very tender and almost all the liquid has gone.

2. Stir in the lentils and canned tomatoes, and season with salt and black pepper. Simmer, uncovered, for 15 minutes or until thick. Stir in sugar to taste. Remove from the heat.

3. Ladle out a quarter of the mixture and puree in a food processor or blender. Combine the pureed and unpureed portions. Serve with yogurt and rice.

* This recipe is not suitable for children because it contains alcohol.

COOK'S TIP

Oil-water spray is far lower in calories than oil alone and, because it sprays on thinly and evenly, you'll use less. Fill one-eighth of a travel-size spray bottle with oil, such as sunflower, light olive, or vegetable (canola) oil, and then fill up with water. To use, shake well before spraying. Store in the refrigerator.

Chili Bean Cake

Preparation Time 10 minutes • Cooking Time 10 minutes • Serves 4 • Per Serving 265 calories, 6g fat (1g saturated), 41g carbohydrates, 2,100mg sodium • Easy

3 tablespoons olive oil

1⅓ cups whole-wheat bread crumbs

1 bunch of scallions, finely chopped

1 orange bell pepper, seeded and chopped

1 small green chili, seeded and finely chopped (see Cook's Tip on page 13)

1 garlic clove, crushed

1 teaspoon ground turmeric (optional)

2 cups canned mixed beans (such as kidney beans, navy beans, and chickpeas), drained and rinsed

3 tablespoons mayonnaise

½ bunch fresh basil, chopped

salt and ground black pepper

sour cream and freshly chopped cilantro to serve

lime wedges (optional)

1. Heat 2 tablespoons of oil in a nonstick skillet over medium heat and sauté the bread crumbs until golden brown and beginning to crisp. Remove and put to one side.

2. Add the remaining oil to the skillet and sauté the scallions until soft and golden brown. Add the orange bell pepper, chili, garlic, and turmeric, if using. Cook, stirring for 5 minutes.

3. Add the beans, mayonnaise, two-thirds of the fried bread crumbs, and the basil. Season with salt and black pepper, mash roughly with a fork, and then press the mixture down to flatten and sprinkle with the remaining bread crumbs. Cook the bean cake over medium heat for 4–5 minutes, until the bottom is golden brown. Remove from the heat, cut into wedges, and serve with sour cream, cilantro, and the lime wedges, if desired.

Curried Tofu Burgers

Preparation Time 20 minutes • Cooking Time 6–8 minutes • Serves 4 • Per Serving 253 calories, 18g fat (3g saturated), 15g carbohydrates, 200mg sodium • Dairy Free • Easy

1 tablespoon sunflower oil, plus extra to fry
1 large carrot, finely grated
1 large onion, finely grated
2 teaspoons coriander seeds, finely crushed (optional)
1 garlic clove, crushed
1 teaspoon curry paste (see Cook's Tip on page 83)
1 teaspoon tomato paste
8 ounces firm tofu
½ cup fresh whole-wheat bread crumbs
¼ cup mixed nuts, finely chopped
all-purpose flour to dust
salt and ground black pepper
rice and green vegetables to serve

1. Heat the oil in a large skillet. Add the carrot and onion, and sauté for 3–4 minutes, until the vegetables are softened, stirring all the time. Add the coriander seeds, if using, the garlic, curry paste, and tomato paste. Increase the heat and cook for 2 minutes, stirring all the time.

2. Put the tofu into a bowl and mash with a potato masher. Stir in the vegetables, bread crumbs, and nuts. Season with salt and black pepper. Beat thoroughly until the mixture starts to stick together. With floured hands, shape the mixture into eight patties.

3. Heat some oil in a skillet and pan-fry the burgers for 3–4 minutes on each side until golden brown. Alternatively, brush lightly with oil and cook under a hot broiler for about 3 minutes on each side or until golden brown. Drain on paper towels and serve hot, with rice and green vegetables.

Black-Eyed Pea Chili

Preparation Time 10 minutes • Cooking Time 20 minutes • Serves 4 • Per Serving 245 calories,
5g fat (1g saturated), 39g carbohydrates, 1,800mg sodium • Easy

- **1 tablespoon olive oil**
- **1 onion, chopped**
- **3 celery sticks, finely chopped**
- **2 (15-ounce) cans black-eyed peas,
  drained and rinsed**
- **2 (14½-ounce) cans diced tomatoes**
- **2 or 3 splashes of Tabasco sauce**
- **3 tablespoons freshly chopped
  cilantro**
- **4 warmed tortillas and sour cream
  to serve**

1. Heat the oil in a skillet. Add the onion and celery and cook for 10 minutes, until softened.

2. Add the beans, tomatoes, and Tabasco to the skillet. Bring to a boil. Then reduce the heat and simmer for 10 minutes.

3. Just before serving, stir in the cilantro. Spoon the chili onto the warm tortillas, roll up, and serve with sour cream.

TRY SOMETHING DIFFERENT
Replace half the black-eyed peas with red kidney beans.

Spiced Bean and Vegetable Stew

Preparation Time 5 minutes • Cooking Time about 30 minutes • Serves 6 • Per Serving 262 calories, 7g fat (1g saturated), 44g carbohydrates, 1,300mg sodium • Gluten Free • Dairy Free • Easy

3 tablespoons olive oil
2 small onions, sliced
2 garlic cloves, crushed
1 tablespoon sweet paprika
1 small dried red chili, seeded and finely chopped
3 large sweet potatoes, peeled and cubed (about 5 cups)
1 butternut squash (or 4 cups pumpkin), peeled, seeded, and cubed

4 ounces okra, trimmed
2 cups canned tomato puree or tomato sauce
3½ cups water
1 (15-ounce) can navy or cannellini beans, drained and rinsed
salt and ground black pepper

1. Heat the oil in a large, heavy saucepan over very gentle heat. Add the onion and garlic and cook for 5 minutes. Stir in the paprika and chili, and cook for another 2 minutes.

2. Add the sweet potatoes, butternut squash or pumpkin, okra, canned tomato puree or sauce, and the water. Season generously with salt and black pepper. Cover and bring to a boil. Then reduce the heat and simmer for 20 minutes or until the vegetables are tender.

3. Add the navy or cannellini beans and cook for 3 minutes to warm through. Serve immediately.

Mixed Beans with Lemon Vinaigrette

Preparation Time 15 minutes • Serves 6 • Per Serving 285 calories, 19g fat (3g saturated), 22g carbohydrates, 1,000mg sodium • Gluten Free • Dairy Free • Easy

2 cups canned mixed beans (such as kidney beans, navy beans, and cannellini beans), drained and rinsed

1 (15-ounce) can chickpeas, drained and rinsed

2 shallots, finely chopped

2 tablespoons lemon juice

2 teaspoons honey

½ cup extra virgin olive oil

3 tablespoons freshly chopped mint

¼ cup freshly chopped Italian parsley

fresh mint sprigs and lemon zest to garnish

salt and ground black pepper

1. Put the beans and chickpeas into a bowl and add the shallots.

2. To make the vinaigrette, whisk together the lemon juice, honey, and salt and black pepper to taste. Gradually whisk in the oil and stir in the chopped herbs. Just before serving, pour the dressing over the bean mixture and toss well.

3. Transfer the salad to a serving dish, garnish with mint sprigs and lemon zest, and serve immediately.

GET AHEAD

To prepare ahead Complete the recipe to the end of step 2 but don't add the herbs to the vinaigrette. Cover and chill for up to two days. *To use* Remove from the refrigerator up to 1 hour before serving, stir in the herbs, and complete the recipe.

Roasted Tomato Bulgur Salad

Preparation Time 10 minutes, plus soaking • Cooking Time 10–15 minutes • Serves 6 •
Per Serving 225 calories, 15g fat (2g saturated), 19g carbohydrates, trace sodium • Dairy Free • Easy

1¼ cups bulgur wheat (see Cook's Tip)
5 cups cherry tomatoes or baby plum tomatoes (about 1½ pounds)
½ cup extra virgin olive oil
a handful each of fresh mint and basil, coarsely chopped, plus fresh basil sprigs to garnish
3–4 tablespoons balsamic vinegar
1 bunch of scallions, sliced
salt and ground black pepper

1. Put the bulgur wheat into a bowl and add boiling water to cover by ½ inch. Cover and soak for 30 minutes.

2. Preheat the oven to 425°F. Put the tomatoes into a small roasting pan, drizzle with half the oil, and add half the mint. Season with salt and black pepper and roast for 10–15 minutes, until they begin to soften.

3. Put the remaining oil and the vinegar into a large bowl. Add the warm pan juices from the roasted tomatoes and the bulgur wheat.

4. Stir in the remaining chopped herbs and the scallions and check the seasoning. You may need a little more vinegar, depending on the sweetness of the tomatoes.

5. Add the tomatoes and carefully toss to combine. Serve garnished with basil sprigs.

COOK'S TIP

Bulgur wheat is widely used in Middle Eastern cooking and has a light, nutty flavor and texture. It is available in several different sizes— from coarse to fine.

Summer Couscous

Preparation Time 10 minutes • Cooking Time 20 minutes • Serves 4 • Per Serving 405 calories,
21g fat (3g saturated), 49g carbohydrates, trace sodium • Dairy Free • Easy

1 cup baby plum tomatoes, halved
2 small eggplants, thickly sliced
2 large yellow bell peppers, seeded
 and coarsely chopped
2 red onions, cut into thin wedges
2 fat garlic cloves, crushed
⅓ cup olive oil
1½ cups couscous
1¼ cups cold water
1 (14½-ounce) can diced tomatoes
2 tablespoons harissa paste
2 tablespoons toasted pumpkin
 seeds (optional)
1 large bunch of fresh cilantro,
 coarsely chopped
salt and ground black pepper

1. Preheat the oven to 450°F.
Put the vegetables and garlic into
a large roasting pan, drizzle
3 tablespoons oil over them, and
season with salt and black pepper.
Toss to coat. Roast for 20 minutes
or until tender.

2. Meanwhile, put the couscous
into a separate roasting pan and
add the cold water. Let soak for
5 minutes. Stir in the tomatoes
and harissa, and drizzle with the
remaining oil. Put into the oven next
to the vegetables for 4–5 minutes to
warm through.

3. Stir the pumpkin seeds, if
desired, and the cilantro into the
couscous and season. Add
the vegetables and stir through.

Wild Mushroom Risotto

Preparation Time 10 minutes • Cooking Time about 30 minutes • Serves 6 • Per Serving 341 calories, 12g fat (2g saturated), 48g carbohydrates, trace sodium • Gluten Free • Dairy Free • Easy

3½ cups vegetable stock

⅓ cup olive oil

2 shallots, finely chopped

2 garlic cloves, finely chopped

2 teaspoons freshly chopped thyme, plus sprigs to garnish

1 teaspoon grated lemon zest

1⅔ cups risotto (arborio) rice

⅔ cup dry white wine*

1 pound mixed fresh mushrooms (such as oyster, shiitake, and porcini), sliced if large

1 tablespoon freshly chopped Italian parsley

salt and ground black pepper

1. Heat the stock in a large saucepan to a gentle simmer.

2. Meanwhile, heat half of the oil in a heavy saucepan. Add the shallots, garlic, chopped thyme, and lemon zest, and sauté gently for 5 minutes or until the shallots are softened. Add the rice and stir for 1 minute or until the grains are glossy. Add the wine, bring to a boil, and let simmer until almost totally evaporated.

3. Gradually add the stock to the rice, a ladleful at a time, stirring with each addition and allowing it to be absorbed before adding more. Continue adding the stock slowly until the rice is tender. This should take about 25 minutes.

4. About 5 minutes before the rice is ready, heat the remaining oil in a large skillet and sauté the mushrooms over high heat for 4–5 minutes. Add to the rice with the parsley. The risotto should still be moist; if necessary, add a little more stock. Check the seasoning and serve immediately, garnished with thyme sprigs.

* This recipe is not suitable for children because it contains alcohol.

DOS AND DON'TS FOR THE PERFECT RISOTTO

Always use risotto rice; the grains are thicker and shorter than long-grain rice and have a high starch content. They absorb more liquid slowly, producing a creamy risotto.

Stock should be hot when added; this swells the grains, yet keeps them firm. Keep the stock simmering in a saucepan. Add it ladle by ladle to the risotto, allowing it to be absorbed by the rice after each addition.

The correct heat is vital. If the risotto gets too hot, the liquid evaporates too quickly and the rice won't cook evenly. If the heat is too low, the risotto will turn gluey. Over medium heat, the rice should cook in about 25 minutes.

Don't leave the risotto—stir it constantly to loosen the rice from the bottom of the pan.

The quantity of liquid given is approximate; adjust it so that, when cooked, the rice is tender but firm to the bite. It should be creamily bound together, neither runny nor dry.

Asparagus Risotto

Preparation Time 10 minutes • Cooking Time 25 minutes • Serves 4 • Per Serving 374 calories, 16g fat (10g saturated), 47g carbohydrates, 1,100mg sodium • Gluten Free • Easy

4 tablespoons butter
2 shallots, diced
2 garlic cloves, crushed
1 cup risotto (arborio) rice
2 cups hot vegetable stock
2 tablespoons mascarpone cheese
½ cup finely grated Parmesan
cheese, plus shavings to garnish
(see Cook's Tip on page 18)
2 tablespoons freshly chopped
parsley
1 pound asparagus spears,
blanched and halved

1. Melt the butter in a heavy saucepan, add the shallots and garlic, and sauté over gentle heat until soft.

2. Stir in the rice and cook for 1–2 minutes, and then add the hot stock. Bring to a boil, and then reduce the heat and simmer for 15–20 minutes, stirring occasionally to be sure that the rice isn't sticking. Almost all the stock should be absorbed and the rice should be tender.

3. Add the mascarpone, half of the Parmesan, and half of the parsley to the pan. Stir in the asparagus and the remaining parsley and Parmesan. Divide among four plates, garnish with shavings of Parmesan, and serve.

Tomato Risotto

Preparation Time 10 minutes • Cooking Time 25–30 minutes • Serves 6 • Per Serving 264 calories, 4g fat (1g saturated), 49g carbohydrates, 500mg sodium • Gluten Free • Easy

1 large fresh rosemary sprig
2 tablespoons olive oil
1 small onion, finely chopped
1²⁄₃ cups risotto (arborio) rice
¼ cup dry white wine*
3 cups hot vegetable stock
2 cups cherry tomatoes, halved
salt and ground black pepper
Parmesan cheese shavings
  (optional, see Cook's Tip on
  page 18), green salad, and extra
  virgin olive oil to serve

1. Pull the leaves from the rosemary and coarsely chop. Set aside.

2. Heat the oil in a flameproof Dutch oven, add the onion, and cook for 8–10 minutes, until the onions begin to soften. Add the rice and stir to coat in the oil and onion. Pour in the wine, and then the hot stock, stirring well to mix.

3. Bring to a boil, stirring, and then reduce the heat, cover, and simmer for 5 minutes. Stir in the tomatoes and chopped rosemary. Simmer, covered, for another 10–15 minutes, until the rice is tender and most of the liquid has been absorbed. Season to taste.

4. Serve immediately with shavings of Parmesan, if desired, a large green salad, and extra virgin olive oil to drizzle over the risotto.

* This recipe is not suitable for children because it contains alcohol.

Squash Risotto with Hazelnut Butter

Preparation Time 15 minutes • Cooking Time 35 minutes • Serves 4 • Per Serving 706 calories, 50g fat (27g saturated), 51g carbohydrates, 1,100mg sodium • Gluten Free • Easy

4 tablespoons butter

1 medium onion, finely chopped

1 butternut squash, halved, peeled, seeded, and cut into small cubes (see Cook's Tip)

2 garlic cloves, crushed

1 cup risotto rice

2½ cups hot vegetable stock

grated zest of ½ orange

1½ ounces Parmesan, shaved (see Cook's Tip on page 18)

salt and ground black pepper

FOR THE HAZELNUT BUTTER

⅓ cup hazelnuts

½ cup (1 stick) butter, softened

2 tablespoons freshly chopped Italian parsley

1. To make the hazelnut butter, spread the hazelnuts on a baking sheet and toast under a hot broiler until golden brown, turning frequently. Put the nuts in a clean dish towel and rub off the skins, and then chop finely. Put the nuts, butter, and parsley on a piece of wax paper. Season with pepper and mix together. Mold into a sausage shape, twist the wax paper at both ends, and chill.

2. To make the risotto, melt the butter in a large pan and sauté the onion until soft but not brown. Add the squash and sauté over low heat for 5–8 minutes, until just beginning to soften. Add the garlic and rice, and stir until well mixed. Increase the heat to medium and add the hot stock a little at a time, allowing the liquid to be absorbed after each addition. This will take about 25 minutes.

3. Stir in the orange zest and Parmesan, and season with salt and pepper. Serve the risotto with a slice of the hazelnut butter melting on top.

COOK'S TIP

You can substitute other types of squash for the butternut squash, such as acorn or kabocha.

Cheesy Polenta with Tomato Sauce

Preparation Time 15 minutes, plus cooling • Cooking Time 45 minutes • Serves 4 • Per Serving 249 calories, 9g fat (4g saturated), 31g carbohydrates, 900mg sodium • Gluten Free • Easy

oil to grease
4½ cups water
1½ cups polenta
¼ cup freshly chopped herbs, such as oregano, chives, and Italian parsley
1 cup freshly grated Parmesan cheese (see Cook's Tip on page 18), plus fresh Parmesan shavings to serve
salt and ground black pepper

FOR THE TOMATO AND BASIL SAUCE
1 tablespoon vegetable oil
3 garlic cloves, crushed
2 cups tomato puree or tomato sauce
1 bay leaf
1 fresh thyme sprig
large pinch of sugar
3 tablespoons freshly chopped basil, plus extra to garnish

1. Lightly oil a 10 × 7-inch dish. Bring the water and ¼ teaspoon salt to a boil in a large saucepan. Sprinkle in the polenta, whisking constantly. Reduce the heat and simmer, stirring frequently, for 10–15 minutes, until the mixture leaves the sides of the pan.

2. Stir in the herbs and Parmesan and season to taste with salt and black pepper. Spoon into the prepared dish and let cool.

3. Next, make the tomato and basil sauce. Heat the oil in a saucepan and sauté the garlic for 30 seconds (do not brown). Add the tomato puree or sauce, the bay leaf, thyme, and sugar. Season with salt and black pepper, bring to a boil, and then reduce the heat and simmer uncovered for 5–10 minutes. Remove the bay leaf and thyme sprig and add the chopped basil.

4. To serve, cut the polenta into pieces and lightly brush with oil. Preheat a ridged grill pan and cook for 3–4 minutes on each side, or broil under a preheated broiler for 7–8 minutes on each side. Serve with the tomato and basil sauce, fresh Parmesan shavings, and chopped basil.

GET AHEAD
To prepare ahead Complete the recipe to the end of step 3. Cover and chill separately for up to two days.
To use Complete the recipe.

Grilled Polenta with Gorgonzola Salad

Preparation Time 20 minutes, plus cooling • Cooking Time 20 minutes • Serves 4 • Per Serving 362 calories, 22g fat (11g saturated), 28g carbohydrates, 1,100mg sodium • Gluten Free • Easy

2 tablespoons olive oil, plus extra to grease
1¼ cups low-fat milk
10 fresh sage leaves, coarsely chopped
1¼ cups water
¾ cup instant polenta
2 garlic cloves, crushed
2 tablespoons butter
3½ cups salad greens
4 ounces Gorgonzola, cut into cubes (see Cook's Tip on page 18)
1 cup sun-dried tomatoes in oil, drained
⅔ cup roasted red peppers, drained
salt and ground black pepper

1. Lightly oil an 8½-inch loaf pan. Pour the milk into a saucepan. Then add the sage, 1 teaspoon of salt, and the water and bring to a boil. Add the polenta to the pan in a thin steady stream, stirring to make a smooth paste.

2. Reduce the heat, add the garlic, and cook for about 8 minutes, stirring occasionally. Add the oil. Then season with black pepper and stir well. Press into the prepared loaf pan, smooth the top, and let cool for 45 minutes.

3. Once the polenta is cool, turn it out onto a board and cut into eight slices.

4. Melt the butter in a ridged griddle pan and cook the polenta slices on each side until golden brown. Divide among four plates. Add the salad greens, Gorgonzola, sun-dried tomatoes, and roasted peppers, and serve.

PASTAS AND PIZZAS

Artichoke and Mushroom Lasagna

Preparation Time 25 minutes • Cooking Time about 1½ hours • Serves 6 • Per Serving 322 calories, 21g fat (11g saturated), 19g carbohydrates, 700mg sodium • Easy

3 tablespoons olive oil

2 onions, coarsely chopped

3 garlic cloves, crushed

¼ cup walnuts

2½ pounds mixed mushrooms (such as brown-cap and white), coarsely chopped

8 cherry tomatoes

4 tablespoons butter, plus extra to grease

⅓ cup all-purpose flour

4½ cups full-fat milk

2 bay leaves

2 tablespoons lemon juice

8 ounces freshly prepared noodles or oven-ready lasagna noodles

1 (14-ounce) can artichoke hearts in water, drained and halved

¾ cup freshly grated Parmesan cheese (see Cook's Tip on page 18)

salt and ground black pepper

fresh oregano sprigs to garnish (optional)

1. Heat the oil in a large skillet and sauté the onions gently for 10 minutes, until soft. Add the garlic and walnuts and sauté for 3–4 minutes, until pale golden. Stir in the mushrooms and cook for 10 minutes. Simmer briskly for another 10 minutes or until all the liquid has evaporated. Add the tomatoes to the skillet, and then remove from the heat and set aside.

2. Preheat the oven to 400°F. Melt the butter in a saucepan, add the flour, and stir over gentle heat for 1 minute. Slowly whisk in the milk until you have a smooth mixture. Bring to a boil, add the bay leaves, and then stir over a gentle heat for 10 minutes or until thickened and smooth. Add the lemon juice and season to taste with salt and black pepper. Discard the bay leaves.

3. Grease a shallow ovenproof dish and layer lasagna noodles over the bottom. Spoon half of the mushroom mixture over the noodles, and then half of the artichokes. Cover with a layer of lasagna noodles and half of the sauce. Spoon the remaining mushroom mixture over the top, and then add the remaining artichokes. Top with the remaining lasagna noodles. Stir the Parmesan into the remaining sauce and spoon evenly over the top of the lasagna.

4. Bake in the oven for 40–50 minutes, until golden brown and bubbling. Garnish with oregano sprigs, if using, and serve.

GET AHEAD

To prepare ahead Complete the recipe to the end of step 3. Then cool, cover, and chill for up to three hours.

To use Remove from the refrigerator about 30 minutes before cooking, and then complete the recipe.

Mixed Mushroom Cannelloni

Preparation Time 15 minutes • Cooking Time 50–55 minutes • Serves 4 • Per Serving 631 calories, 37g fat (18g saturated), 50g carbohydrates, 1,900mg sodium • A Little Effort

6 lasagna noodles (see Cook's Tip)
3 tablespoons olive oil
1 small onion, finely sliced
3 garlic cloves, sliced
½ cup freshly chopped thyme
8 ounces cremini or brown-cap
  mushrooms, coarsely chopped
4 ounces flat-cap mushrooms,
  coarsely chopped
2 (4-ounce) goat cheese logs, with
  rind (see Cook's Tip on page 18)
1½ cups prepared cheese sauce
  (see Cook's Tip on page 138)
salt and ground black pepper
green salad to serve

1. Preheat the oven to 350°F. Cook the lasagna in boiling water until just tender. Drain well and run it under cold water to cool. Keep covered with cold water until ready to use.

2. Heat the oil in a large skillet and add the onion. Cook over medium heat for 7–10 minutes, until the onion is soft. Add the garlic and sauté for 1–2 minutes. Put a few slices of garlic and a little thyme to one side. Add the rest to the pan with the mushrooms. Cook for another 5 minutes or until the mushrooms are golden brown and there is no excess liquid in the pan. Season, remove from the heat, and put to one side.

3. Crumble one of the goat cheese logs into the cooled mushroom mixture and stir together. Drain the lasagna noodles and pat dry with paper towels. Spoon 2–3 tablespoons of the mushroom mixture along the length of each each lasagna noodle, half an inch from the edge. Roll up the pasta noodles and cut each roll in half.

4. Put the pasta into a shallow, ovenproof dish and spoon the cheese sauce over it. Slice the remaining goat cheese into thick circles and arrange across the middle of the pasta rolls. Sprinkle the reserved garlic and thyme on top. Cook in the oven for 30–35 minutes, until golden brown and bubbling. Serve with a green salad.

COOK'S TIP

Fresh lasagna noodles wrapped around a filling are used here to make cannelloni, but you can also buy cannelloni tubes, which can be filled easily using a teaspoon.

Macaroni and Cheese

Preparation Time 5 minutes • Cooking Time 15 minutes • Serves 4 • Per Serving 1137 calories, 69g fat (44g saturated), 96g carbohydrates, 2,000mg sodium • Easy

1 pound macaroni
2 cups crème fraîche
1¾ cups freshly grated Parmesan cheese (see Cook's Tip on page 18)
2 tablespoons prepared English or Dijon mustard
⅓ cup freshly chopped Italian parsley
ground black pepper
green salad to serve

1. Cook the macaroni in a large saucepan of lightly salted boiling water according to the package directions. Drain and keep to one side.

2. Preheat the broiler to high. Put the crème fraîche into a saucepan and heat gently. Stir in 1½ cups Parmesan, the mustard, and the parsley, and season well with black pepper.

3. Stir the pasta into the sauce, spoon into bowls, and sprinkle with the remaining cheese. Broil until golden brown and serve immediately with salad.

Pasta Shells Stuffed with Spinach and Ricotta

Preparation Time 10 minutes • Cooking Time about 45 minutes • Serves 4 • Per Serving 430 calories, 17g fat (7g saturated), 50g carbohydrates, 1,600mg sodium • Easy

1 pound fresh spinach, washed

½ cup ricotta cheese (see Cook's Tip on page 18)

1 large egg

a pinch of freshly grated nutmeg

grated zest of ½ lemon

½ cup freshly grated Parmesan cheese

8 ounces conchiglione pasta shells

½ quantity of Classic Tomato Sauce (see Cook's Tip)

¼ cup pine nuts

salt and ground black pepper

1. Put the spinach into a large saucepan. Cover and cook over low to medium heat for 2–3 minutes, until wilted. Drain, squeeze out the excess liquid, and chop finely.

2. Put the spinach into a large bowl with the ricotta and beat in the egg. Stir in the grated nutmeg, lemon zest, and ¼ cup grated Parmesan and season.

3. Preheat the oven to 400°F. Meanwhile, cook the pasta according to the package directions for oven-baked dishes. Drain well.

4. Spread the Classic Tomato Sauce in the bottom of a 7 × 9-inch ovenproof dish. Fill the shells with the spinach mixture and arrange on top of the sauce. Sprinkle with the remaining grated Parmesan and the pine nuts. Cook in the oven for 20–25 minutes, until golden.

COOK'S TIP

Classic Tomato Sauce

Heat 1 tablespoon olive oil in a saucepan. Add 1 small chopped onion, 1 shredded carrot, and 1 chopped celery stick. Then sauté gently for 20 minutes, until softened. Add 1 crushed garlic clove and ½ tablespoon tomato paste. Cook for 1 minute. Stir in 2 (14½-ounce) cans of plum tomatoes. Then add 1 bay leaf, ½ teaspoon dried oregano, and 2 teaspoons sugar, and simmer for 30 minutes, until thickened. Serves 4.

Pappardelle with Spinach

Preparation Time 5 minutes • Cooking Time 12 minutes • Serves 4 • Per Serving 404 calories, 11g fat (3g saturated), 67g carbohydrates, 300mg sodium • Easy

12 ounces pappardelle pasta
1 (12-ounce) package baby spinach, coarsely chopped
2 tablespoons olive oil
⅓ cup ricotta cheese (see Cook's Tip on page 18)
freshly grated nutmeg
salt and ground black pepper

1. Cook the pappardelle in a large saucepan of lightly salted boiling water according to the package directions until al dente.

2. Drain the pasta well, return to the pan, and add the spinach, oil, and ricotta, tossing for 10–15 seconds, until the spinach has wilted. Season with a little nutmeg, salt, and black pepper, and serve immediately.

Tomato and Artichoke Pasta

Preparation Time 10 minutes • Cooking Time 10–12 minutes • Serves 4 •
Per Serving 380 calories, 11g fat (4g saturated), 59g carbohydrates, 1,300mg sodium • Easy

12 ounces penne pasta

6 pieces sun-dried tomatoes in oil

1 red onion, sliced

about 10 pieces roasted artichoke hearts in oil, drained and coarsely chopped

¼ cup ripe black olives, pitted and coarsely chopped

½ cup grated pecorino cheese (see Cook's Tip on page 18)

3½ cups arugula

1. Cook the pasta in a large saucepan of lightly salted boiling water according to the package directions until al dente. Drain well.

2. Meanwhile, drain the sun-dried tomatoes, reserving the oil, and coarsely chop. Heat 1 tablespoon oil from the tomatoes in a large skillet, add the onion, and sauté for 5–6 minutes, until softened and turning golden. Add the tomatoes, artichokes, and olives to the skillet and heat for 3–4 minutes, until hot.

3. Add half the pecorino cheese and stir through. Remove from the heat and stir in the arugula and pasta. Divide the pasta among four bowls and sprinkle the remaining pecorino over the top to serve.

Fusilli with Chili and Tomatoes

Preparation Time 5 minutes • Cooking Time 15 minutes • Serves 4 • Per Serving 738 calories, 38g fat (10g saturated), 74g carbohydrates, 1,000mg sodium • Easy

12 ounces fusilli or other short pasta
4 tablespoons olive oil
1 large red chili, seeded and finely chopped (see Cook's Tip on page 13)
1 garlic clove, crushed
18 ounces cherry tomatoes
2 tablespoons freshly chopped basil
2 ounces Parmesan cheese shavings (see Cook's Tip on page 18)
salt and ground black pepper

1. Cook the pasta in a large saucepan of lightly salted boiling water according to the package directions until al dente. Drain.

2. Meanwhile, heat the oil in a large skillet over high heat. Add the chili and garlic, and cook for 30 seconds. Add the tomatoes, season with salt and pepper, and cook over high heat for 3 minutes or until the skins begin to split.

3. Add the basil and drained pasta and toss together. Transfer to a serving dish, sprinkle the Parmesan shavings over the top, and serve immediately.

Pesto Gnocchi

Preparation Time 10 minutes • Cooking Time 10 minutes • Serves 4 • Per Serving 481 calories, 24g fat (6g saturated), 56g carbohydrates, 400mg sodium • Easy

1¾ pounds fresh gnocchi

2 cups green beans, trimmed and chopped

½ cup fresh pesto (see Cook's Tip on page 14)

10 sun-dried tomatoes, coarsely chopped

1. Cook the gnocchi in a large saucepan of lightly salted boiling water according to the package directions or until all the gnocchi have floated to the surface. Add the beans to the water for the last 3 minutes of cooking time.

2. Drain the gnocchi and beans, and return to the pan. Add the pesto and tomatoes and toss well. Serve immediately.

Four-Cheese Gnocchi

Bland & pasty (w/o much flavor)

Preparation Time 3 minutes • Cooking Time 10 minutes • Serves 2 • Per Serving 630 calories, 28g fat (15g saturated), 77g carbohydrates, trace sodium • Easy

12 ounces fresh gnocchi

1½ cups prepared four-cheese sauce (see Cook's Tip on page 18)

2 (3½-ounce) packages sun-dried tomatoes

2 tablespoons freshly torn basil leaves, plus basil sprigs to garnish

1 tablespoon freshly grated Parmesan cheese

1 tablespoon butter, chopped

salt and ground black pepper

salad to serve

1. Cook the gnocchi in a large saucepan of lightly salted boiling water according to the package directions or until all the gnocchi have floated to the surface. Drain well and put the gnocchi back into the pan.

2. Preheat the broiler. Add the four-cheese sauce and tomatoes to the gnocchi and heat gently, stirring, for 2 minutes.

3. Season with salt and black pepper. Then add the basil and stir again. Spoon into individual heatproof bowls, sprinkle a little Parmesan over each one, and dot with butter.

4. Cook under the broiler for 3–5 minutes until golden brown and bubbling. Garnish with basil sprigs and serve with salad.

Garlic Cheese Pizza

Preparation Time 20 minutes • Cooking Time 30 minutes • Serves 4 • Per Serving 536 calories, 30g fat (9g saturated), 54g carbohydrates, 600mg sodium • Easy

1½ (6½-ounce) packages pizza crust mix

all-purpose flour to dust

1¼ cups garlic and herb cream cheese (see Cook's Tip on page 18)

12 whole sun-dried tomatoes, drained of oil and cut into rough pieces

¼ cup pine nuts

12 fresh basil leaves

3 tablespoons olive oil

green salad to serve

1. Preheat the oven to 425°F. Put a pizza stone or large baking sheet in the oven to heat up.

2. Mix the pizza crust dough according to the package directions. Place it on a lightly floured work surface and knead for a few minutes or until smooth. Roll out to a 13-inch circle. Transfer the dough to the preheated pizza stone or baking sheet. Pinch a lip around the edge.

3. Crumble the cheese over the dough and flatten with a spatula. Then sprinkle on the sun-dried tomatoes, pine nuts, and basil.

4. Drizzle with the oil and bake for 20–30 minutes, until pale golden and cooked to the center. Serve with a green salad.

TRY SOMETHING DIFFERENT

Use goat cheese instead of garlic and herb cream cheese.

Deli Pizza

Preparation Time 5 minutes • Cooking Time 15 minutes • Serves 4 • Per Serving 440 calories, 15g fat (5g saturated), 64g carbohydrates, 2,800mg sodium • Easy

⅓ cup tomato pizza sauce

2 pizzeria-style pizza crusts

4 ounces soft goat cheese (see Cook's Tip on page 18)

1 red onion, finely sliced

2 cups sun-dried tomatoes

½ cup ripe black olives, pitted

a handful of fresh basil, coarsely torn

green salad to serve

1. Preheat the oven to 425°F. Put a large baking sheet on the top shelf to heat up.

2. Spread a thin layer of the tomato sauce over each of the pizza crusts, leaving a 1-inch border around the edge. Top with dollops of goat cheese. Then sprinkle the red onion, tomatoes, and olives over it.

3. Slide one of the pizzas onto the hot baking sheet and bake for 15 minutes or until golden brown and crisp. Repeat with the second pizza crust. Sprinkle the torn basil over each pizza and serve immediately with a green salad.

TRY SOMETHING DIFFERENT

Try marinated red peppers, artichokes, or chargrilled eggplants instead of olives and sun-dried tomatoes.

SAVORY PIES
AND PASTRIES

Easy Leek Pie

Preparation Time 15 minutes, plus freezing • Cooking Time 1 hour • Serves 6 • Per Serving 571 calories, 39g fat (20g saturated), 45g carbohydrates, 700mg sodium • Easy

2 cups all-purpose flour, plus extra to dust

1 teaspoon dry English mustard

¾ cup (1½ sticks) cold butter, cut into cubes

½ cup shredded sharp cheddar (see Cook's Tip on page 18)

2 egg yolks, lightly beaten

5–6 tablespoons cold water

2 pounds leeks, cut into ½-inch slices, washed, and drained

2 medium red onions, each cut into 8 wedges

juice of ½ lemon

leaves of 5 fresh thyme sprigs

¼ cup olive oil

1 medium egg, lightly beaten

salt and ground black pepper

1. Put the flour, dry mustard, butter, and ½ teaspoon salt into a food processor. Pulse until the mixture forms crumbs, and then add the cheese, egg yolks, and 2–3 tablespoons cold water. Process briefly until the dough comes together. Form into a ball, wrap in plastic wrap, and put in the freezer for 10 minutes.

2. Preheat the oven to 400°F. Cook the leeks with 3 tablespoons water in a covered saucepan until softened. Drain and set aside. Gently cook the onions and lemon juice in a covered saucepan until softened.

3. Roll out the dough to a 15-inch circle on a large, lightly floured sheet of parchment paper. Lift the paper and dough onto a baking sheet. Put the onions and leeks in the center of the dough, leaving a 3-inch border. Sprinkle with the thyme, season with salt and black pepper, and drizzle with the oil. Fold the dough edges over the filling. Brush the rim with beaten egg. Bake for 50 minutes or until the vegetables are tender.

Spinach and Feta Pie

Preparation Time 40 minutes, plus cooling • Cooking Time 45 minutes • Serves 10 • Per Serving 311 calories, 15g fat (9g saturated), 33g carbohydrates, 1,700mg sodium • Easy

1 tablespoon vegetable oil

1 onion, finely chopped

1 garlic clove, crushed

1 tablespoon cumin seeds

1 (12-ounce) bag baby spinach

10 russet potatoes (about
   2½ pounds), boiled until tender,
   cooled, peeled, and sliced

12 ounces feta cheese, crumbled
   (see Cook's Tip on page 18)

2 large eggs, beaten

10 sheets phyllo pastry, thawed
   if frozen

4 tablespoons butter, melted

salt and ground black pepper

1. Heat the oil in a large saucepan and sauté the onion for 10 minutes, until soft. Add the garlic and cumin and cook for 1–2 minutes. Add the spinach, cover, and cook until the spinach has just wilted, about 1–2 minutes. Transfer to a bowl and let cool. Add the potatoes, cheese, and eggs. Then season and mix.

2. Preheat the oven to 400°F. Lightly butter an 11-inch tart pan. Unroll the pastry and cut the sheets lengthwise into thirds. Work with one-third of the strips at a time and cover the remainder with plastic wrap. Lay a strip on the pan, starting from the middle so that half covers the pan and half hangs over the edge, and brush with melted butter. Lay another strip next to it, slightly overlapping, and brush again. Repeat, working quickly around the pan in a cartwheel shape.

3. Add the filling and level the surface. Fold in the overhanging pastry to cover the mixture, filling any gaps with leftover pastry. Drizzle with the remaining melted butter. Bake for 45 minutes or until golden brown.

Winter Roasted Vegetable Tart

Preparation Time 30 minutes • Cooking Time 2 hours • Serves 4 • Per Serving 540 calories, 24g fat (1g saturated), 85g carbohydrates, 500mg sodium • Easy

1 rolled pie crust dough, removed from refrigerator 5 minutes before using

1 small red onion, cut into six wedges

1 raw baby beet, peeled and thickly sliced

1 baby eggplant, quartered

1 small red apple, quartered, cored, and cut into chunky slices

1 garlic clove, crushed

juice of ½ lemon

1 teaspoon freshly chopped thyme

1 tablespoon olive oil

⅓ cup Cranberry and Red Onion Marmalade (see Cook's Tip)

1 cup sliced cremini mushrooms

5 cooked and peeled (or vacuum-packed) chestnuts, chopped

1 tablespoon red currant jelly, warmed

salt and ground black pepper

1. Preheat the oven to 400°F. Put a 4½ × 8-inch loose-bottom rectangular tart pan on a baking sheet. Line the pan with the dough. Then line the dough with parchment paper, fill with pie weights or dried beans, and bake for 15–20 minutes. Remove the paper and weights, prick the bottom of the pastry all over with a fork, and bake for another 5–10 minutes, until golden brown. Cool and remove from the pan.

2. Put the onion, beet, eggplant, apple, and garlic into a roasting pan. Squeeze the lemon juice over the contents, sprinkle with the thyme, and drizzle with oil. Then roast for 20 minutes. Transfer to a bowl and let cool.

3. Put the cooked pastry shell on a baking sheet. Spoon the Cranberry and Red Onion Marmalade over the bottom. Arrange the roasted vegetables and mushrooms on top. Sprinkle the chestnuts on top and season. Brush warmed red currant jelly over the vegetables and cook for 20 minutes. Serve hot.

COOK'S TIP

Cranberry and Red Onion Marmalade

Heat 2 tablespoons olive oil in a pan and gently sauté 2 sliced red onions for 5 minutes. Add the juice of 1 orange, 1 tablespoon pickling spice, ¾ cup packed dark brown sugar, and ⅔ cup ruby port. Then simmer gently for 40 minutes. Add 4½ cups fresh cranberries and cook over medium heat for 20 minutes. Cool and chill for up to two days. This recipe is not suitable for children because it contains alcohol.

Roasted Vegetable Tartlets

Preparation Time 15 minutes • Cooking Time about 7 minutes • Makes 6 • Per Serving 356 calories, 24g fat (1g saturated), 30g carbohydrates, 1,100mg sodium • Easy

2 sheets ready-to-bake puff pastry, thawed if frozen

all-purpose flour to dust

1 large egg, beaten

2 tablespoons coarse sea salt

11 ounces vegetable antipasti in olive oil, or marinated vegetables in olive oil, if needed

2 tablespoons balsamic vinegar

¾ cup prepared red pepper hummus or other hummus (see Cook's Tip on page 67)

2 cups arugula

salt and ground black pepper

1. Preheat the oven to 425°F. Unroll the puff pastry on a lightly floured surface and cut it into six squares. Put the pastry squares on a large baking sheet and prick each one all over with a fork. Brush the surface with beaten egg and sprinkle the edges with sea salt. Bake for 5–7 minutes, until the pastry is golden brown and cooked through. Press down the center of each tartlet slightly with the back of a spatula.

2. Make the dressing. Pour ¼ cup of oil from the jar of antipasti into a bowl (or use olive oil). Add the vinegar, season with salt and black pepper, mix well, and then set aside.

3. To serve, spread some hummus over the middle of each tartlet. Put the tartlets on individual plates and top with the antipasti or marinated vegetables. Whisk the balsamic vinegar dressing. Add the arugula and toss to coat. Then pile a small handful of leaves on top of each tartlet. Serve immediately.

GET AHEAD

To prepare ahead Complete the recipe to the end of step 1. Let the tartlets cool on a wire rack, and then store in an airtight container. They will keep for up to two days. **To use** Complete the recipe.

Leek and Fennel Tart

Preparation Time 35 minutes, plus chilling • Cooking Time 1¼–1½ hours • Serves 12 • Per Serving 319 calories, 24g fat (13g saturated), 20g carbohydrates, 500mg sodium • Easy

2 cups all-purpose flour
½ cup (1 stick) butter, chilled and cut into cubes
⅔ cup finely grated Parmesan cheese (see Cook's Tip on page 18)
⅓ cup cold water
1 tablespoon sunflower oil
2 large leeks, trimmed and chopped
2 fennel bulbs, chopped
3 large eggs, plus 2 yolks
¾ cup milk
¾ cup heavy cream
1½ tablespoons poppy seeds
a few fresh thyme sprigs, leaves stripped and stems discarded
salt and ground black pepper

1. Pulse the flour and butter in a processor until they resemble bread crumbs. Transfer to a bowl and stir in ⅓ cup Parmesan. Then add the cold water until the dough comes together. Knead lightly, form into a ball, wrap in plastic wrap, and chill for 30 minutes.

2. Heat the oil in a large saucepan, add the leeks and fennel, and then cover and cook over low heat for 15–20 minutes, until soft. Strain off any liquid and let cool.

3. Preheat the oven to 400°F. Roll out the dough and line a 12-inch loose-bottom fluted tart pan. Prick the bottom of the dough, cover with parchment paper, and fill with pie weights or dried beans. Chill for 10 minutes. Bake for 12–15 minutes. Remove the paper and weights and bake for another 8–10 minutes. If the pastry puffs up, push it down. Reduce the oven temperature to 325°F. Mix the eggs, yolks, milk, cream, poppy seeds, and remaining Parmesan, and season. Spoon the leek mixture into the pastry shell. Pour in the egg mixture, sprinkle with thyme, and cook for 40–45 minutes until set. Remove the outside of the pan but leave the tart on the bottom to cool.

FREEZING TIP

To freeze Complete the recipe and let cool. Return the tart to the pan, wrap well, and freeze for up to one month.
To use Thaw at cool room temperature, and then warm through for 15 minutes in an oven preheated to 400°F.

Country Tomato and Parmesan Tart

Preparation Time 40 minutes, plus chilling • Cooking Time 40 minutes • Serves 4 • Per Serving 274 calories, 19g fat (12g saturated), 37g carbohydrates, 900mg sodium • Easy

½ cup all-purpose flour

6 tablespoons butter

1⅓ cups finely grated Parmesan (see Cook's Tip on page 18)

¼ teaspoon cayenne pepper

¼ cup sun-dried tomato paste

¼ cup fresh bread crumbs

2 pounds tomatoes, preferably plum, thickly sliced

1 tablespoon freshly chopped thyme, plus extra sprigs to garnish

salt and ground black pepper

1. Preheat the oven to 350°F. Put the flour, butter, ⅔ cup Parmesan, ½ teaspoon salt, and the cayenne pepper into a food processor and blend until the mixture looks like coarse bread crumbs. Set aside one-third of the mixture, cover, and chill. Press the remaining crumb mixture into the bottom of an 8-inch square, loose-bottom tart pan, using the back of a spoon to spread it out to the edges. Chill for 10 minutes. Cook the crumb crust for 15–20 minutes, until light golden brown. Let cool.

2. Spread the tomato paste over the cooled crumb crust, and then sprinkle with half the bread crumbs. Layer the tomato slices and thyme on top and sprinkle with the remaining bread crumbs, the remaining Parmesan, and the reserved crumb mixture. Season with salt and black pepper.

3. Cook the tart in the oven for another 15–20 minutes, until golden brown. Let cool slightly, cut into portions, and garnish with thyme.

COOK'S TIP

The same mixture can be cooked in a 9-inch round pan.

Chestnut and Butternut Phyllo Pastry

Preparation Time 40 minutes • Cooking Time 45–50 minutes • Serves 4 • Per Serving 408 calories, 22g fat (13g saturated), 49g carbohydrates, 500mg sodium • Easy

½ tablespoon olive oil

6 tablespoons butter

½ onion, finely chopped

5 fresh rosemary sprigs

½ small butternut squash, peeled, seeded, and finely chopped

1 celery stick, finely chopped

½ firm pear, finely chopped

9 cooked and peeled (or vacuum-packed) chestnuts, coarsely chopped

2 slices walnut bread, cut into small cubes

8 sheets phyllo pastry

¼ cup cream cheese (see Cook's Tip on page 18)

salt and ground black pepper

1. Heat the oil and 1 tablespoon butter in a medium saucepan, add the onion, and sauté gently for 10 minutes. Finely chop one rosemary sprig and add it with the squash to the pan. Continue to cook for 5 minutes or until everything is soft and golden brown. Add the celery and pear and cook for 1–2 minutes. Add the chestnuts, season, and mix well. Add the bread to the pan, mix everything together, and then set aside to cool.

2. Preheat the oven to 400°F. Melt the remaining butter in a saucepan. Brush one sheet of phyllo pastry with the melted butter and layer another sheet of pastry on top, diagonally. Put a quarter of the chestnut mixture in the center of the pastry and dot with a quarter of the cream cheese. Brush the edges of the pastry with a little more butter, bring the edges up and over the filling, and pinch together tightly to make a package. Repeat to make three more packages.

3. Put the packages on a lightly greased baking sheet and cook for 25–30 minutes, until the pastry is golden brown and the filling is piping hot. Five minutes before the end of the cooking time, put a rosemary sprig into the top of each package. Serve hot.

FREEZING TIP

To freeze Complete the recipe to the end of step 2, put the pastry in a freezeproof container, and freeze for up to one month.

To use Cook from frozen in a preheated oven at 400°F for 30 minutes, until the pastry is golden. Complete the recipe.

Leek, Artichoke, and Mushroom Croûte

Preparation Time 30 minutes, plus cooling and chilling overnight • Cooking Time 30–35 minutes • Serves 8 •
Per Serving 236 calories, 17g fat (1g saturated), 20g carbohydrates, 400mg sodium • Easy

3 tablespoons olive oil

2 garlic cloves, crushed

4 ounces shiitake mushrooms, sliced

1 tablespoon balsamic vinegar

5 cooked and peeled (or vacuum-packed) chestnuts, coarsely chopped

1½ teaspoons freshly chopped thyme

1 (14-ounce) can artichoke hearts, drained and quartered

4 cups sliced leeks

1 sheet ready-to-bake puff pastry, thawed if frozen

butter to grease

1 large egg, lightly beaten

salt and ground black pepper

cranberry sauce and a little extra virgin olive oil to serve

1. Heat 2 tablespoons of olive oil in a large saucepan and sauté the garlic for 1 minute. Add the mushrooms and cook over low heat for 3 minutes to soften. Add the vinegar, chestnuts, ½ teaspoon of thyme leaves, and the artichokes. Then cook for 1 minute. In a separate saucepan, soften the leeks in the remaining 1 tablespoon of oil for 4 minutes. Transfer to a bowl and let cool for 5 minutes.

2. Unroll the pastry, sprinkle with the remaining thyme, and lightly roll or press the thyme into the pastry. Flip the pastry over so that the herbs are on the underside, and then lightly roll out to a 15 × 10-inch rectangle. Using a sharp knife, cut the pastry in half to create two long thin rectangles. Spoon half the mushroom mixture down the center of each. Top with the leeks and season. Brush the pastry edges with water, and then fold each side of the pastry up over the filling and seal. Cut both rolls in half and put onto a greased baking sheet. Cover and chill overnight.

3. Preheat the oven to 400°F. Brush the pastry with egg to glaze. Cook for 20 minutes until the pastry is golden. Slice each croûte into six and serve three slices per person, with cranberry sauce and a light drizzle of extra virgin olive oil.

FREEZING TIP

To freeze *Complete the recipe to the end of step 2. Then wrap and freeze for up to one month.*
To use *Cook from frozen in a preheated oven at 400°F for 25 minutes, until the pastry is golden brown. Complete the recipe.*

Wild Mushroom Pot Pie

Preparation Time 1 hour, plus 1 hour chilling and cooling • Cooking Time about 1 hour • Serves 8 •
Per Serving 710 calories, 51g fat (12g saturated), 58g carbohydrates, 1,200mg sodium • Easy

1 pound wild mushrooms
1¼ cups milk
¾ cup heavy cream
2 garlic cloves, crushed
4 russet potatoes, peeled and
**   thinly sliced**
freshly grated nutmeg
4 tablespoons butter
2 teaspoon freshly chopped thyme,
**   plus fresh sprigs to garnish**
2 sheets ready-to-bake puff pastry,
**   thawed if frozen**
flour to dust
1 extra-large egg, beaten
salt and ground black pepper

1. Rinse the mushrooms in cold running water to remove any grit, and then pat dry with paper towels. Coarsely slice.

2. Put the milk and cream into a large, heavy saucepan with the garlic. Bring to a boil and add the potatoes. Bring back to a boil and simmer gently, stirring occasionally, for 15–20 minutes, until the potatoes are tender. Season with salt, black pepper, and nutmeg. Let cool.

3. Melt the butter in a large skillet. When it's sizzling, add the mushrooms and cook over high heat for 5–10 minutes, stirring all the time, until the mushrooms are cooked and the juices have evaporated completely. Season. Stir in the chopped thyme, and then set aside to cool.

4. On a lightly floured surface, roll out the pastry thinly. Cut into eight circles about 5 inches in diameter for the tops, and eight circles about 4½ inches in diameter for the bottoms. Put the smaller pastry circles on baking sheets and brush the edges with beaten egg. Put a large spoonful of the cooled potato mixture in the center of each circle, leaving a ½-inch border around the edge. Top with a spoonful of the mushroom mixture, and cover with the pastry tops. Press the edges together well to seal. Chill for 30 minutes–1 hour.

5. Meanwhile, preheat the oven to 425°F and put two baking trays in to heat up. Use the back of a knife to scallop the edges of the pastry and brush the top with the remaining beaten egg. Use a knife to decorate the tops of the pies, if you desire.

6. Put the pies, on their baking sheets, in the preheated baking trays. Cook for 15–20 minutes, until deep golden brown, swapping the pans around in the oven halfway through cooking. Serve immediately, garnished with thyme sprigs.

GET AHEAD
Complete the recipe to the end of step 4. Then cover and chill overnight until ready to cook.

Red Onion Tart

Preparation Time 15 minutes • Cooking Time 35–40 minutes • Serves 12 • Per Serving 235 calories, 15g fat (3g saturated), 23g carbohydrates, 400mg sodium • Easy

4 tablespoons butter

2 tablespoons olive oil

5 red onions (about 2½ pounds), sliced into circles

1 tablespoon packed light brown sugar

¾ cup white wine*

4 teaspoons white wine vinegar

1 tablespoon freshly chopped thyme, plus extra to garnish (optional)

1 (1-pound) package ready-to-bake puff pastry, thawed if frozen

all-purpose flour to dust

salt and ground black pepper

1. Lightly grease two 9-inch nonstick pie pans with a little of the butter and set aside.

2. Melt the remaining butter with the oil in a large nonstick skillet. Add the onions and sugar, and sauté for 10–15 minutes, until golden brown, keeping the onions in their circles.

3. Preheat the oven to 425°F. Add the wine, vinegar, and thyme to the skillet. Bring to a boil and let it simmer until the liquid has evaporated. Season with salt and black pepper. Then divide the mixture between the pans and let cool.

4. Halve the pastry. On a lightly floured surface, roll out each piece thinly into a circle shape just larger than the pie pan. Put one pastry circle over the onion mixture in each pan and tuck in the edges. Prick the pastry dough all over with a fork.

5. Cook the tarts for 15–20 minutes, until the pastry rises and is golden. Take out of the oven and put a large warm plate over the pastry. Turn the whole thing over and shake gently to release the tart. Then remove the pan. Scatter with thyme, if desired, and cut into wedges to serve.

* This recipe is not suitable for children because it contains alcohol.

GET AHEAD

To prepare ahead Complete the recipe to the end of step 4. Cover and keep in the refrigerator for up to 24 hours.
To use Complete the recipe.

Spinach and Goat Cheese in Phyllo

Preparation Time 45 minutes, plus cooling • Cooking Time 10 minutes • Serves 6 • Per Serving 345 calories, 22g fat (12g saturated), 26g carbohydrates, 800mg sodium • Easy

4 cups fresh spinach leaves
2 tablespoons sunflower oil
1 onion, finely chopped
1 large garlic clove, chopped
9 ounces soft goat cheese (see Cook's Tip on page 18)
6 sheets phyllo pastry, thawed if frozen
4 tablespoons butter, melted
sesame seeds to sprinkle
salt and ground black pepper

1. Plunge the spinach into a saucepan of boiling water, bring back to a boil for 1 minute, and then drain and refresh under cold water. Squeeze out all the excess liquid and chop finely.

2. Heat the oil in a saucepan, add the onion and garlic, and cook until translucent. Then let cool. Combine the spinach, onion mixture, and goat cheese in a bowl, and season generously.

3. Cut the pastry into 24 pieces, roughly 4 inches square. Brush one square with melted butter, cover with a second square, and brush with more butter. Put to one side and cover with a damp dish towel. Repeat with the remaining squares to make twelve sets.

4. Put 2 teaspoonfuls of the filling on each square and join up the corners to form a package. Brush with a little more butter, sprinkle with sesame seeds, and chill for 20 minutes. Meanwhile, preheat the oven to 425°F. Bake for about 5 minutes or until the pastry is crisp and browned.

Mushroom Tarts

Preparation Time 40 minutes, plus chilling • Cooking Time 50 minutes • Serves 6 • Per Serving 659 calories, 48g fat (29g saturated), 37g carbohydrates, 500mg sodium • Easy

1¾ cups all-purpose flour, plus
   extra to dust
⅔ cup (1¼ sticks) chilled butter,
   cubed, plus 4 tablespoons
1 extra-large egg
2 onions, finely chopped
1 pound mixed mushrooms, sliced
1 garlic clove, crushed
½ ounce dried mushrooms, soaked
   in 1¼ cups boiling water for
   10 minutes
1¼ cups medium-dry sherry*
1¼ cups heavy cream
salt and ground black pepper
fresh thyme sprigs to garnish
green salad to serve

1. Process the flour and 1¼ sticks butter in a food processor until the mixture resembles fine bread crumbs. Add the egg and pulse until the mixture comes together. Knead lightly on a floured surface and shape into six balls. Wrap and chill for 30 minutes.

2. Roll out the dough on a lightly floured surface and line six loose-bottom tart pans, 3½ inches across the bottom. Prick the bottoms and chill for 20 minutes.

3. Meanwhile, preheat the oven to 400°F. Line the pastry shell with parchment paper, fill with pie weights or dried beans, and bake for 15–20 minutes. Remove the paper and weights, prick the pastry bottom all over with a fork, and cook for another 5–10 minutes, until golden brown. Reduce the oven temperature to 350°F.

4. To make the filling, heat 4 tablespoons butter in a saucepan, add the onions, and cook for 10 minutes. Add the sliced mushrooms and garlic, and cook for 5 minutes. Then remove and set aside. Put the dried mushrooms and their liquid into the pan with the sherry. Bring to a boil and simmer for 10 minutes. Then add the cream and cook for 5 minutes or until syrupy.

5. To serve, warm the pastry in the oven for 5 minutes. Add the reserved mushrooms to the sauce, season, and heat through. Pour into the pastry shells, garnish with thyme, and serve with salad.

* This recipe is not suitable for children because it contains alcohol

FREEZING TIP
To freeze *Complete the recipe to the end of step 1. Then cool, wrap, and freeze the tarts.*
To use *Thaw, and then complete the recipe.*

Cheese and Egg Tartlets

Preparation Time 15 minutes • Cooking Time 15–20 minutes • Serves 12 • Per Serving 134 calories, 7g fat (3g saturated), 13g carbohydrates, 500mg sodium • Easy

12 thin slices white bread
2 tablespoons butter, melted
2 hard-boiled eggs, finely chopped
½ cup shredded cheddar cheese
　(see Cook's Tip on page 18)
2–3 tablespoons mayonnaise
mustard and microgreen leaves
　(optional)
salt and ground black pepper

1. Preheat the oven to 350°F. Flatten the bread slightly with a rolling pin, and cut out circles with a 3-inch fluted cutter. Brush with melted butter and press into the cups of a muffin pan. Set another muffin pan on top to keep the bread pressed down and bake for 15–20 minutes, until golden brown and crisp. Cool on a wire rack.

2. Mix the hard-boiled eggs with the cheese and mayonnaise. Season with salt and black pepper. Divide among the tartlet shells and sprinkle with the mustard and microgreen leaves, if desired.

GET AHEAD

To prepare ahead Complete the recipe to the end of step 1. Cool and store the tartlet shells in airtight containers for up to two weeks.
To use Complete the recipe.

BREADS, COOKIES, AND CAKES

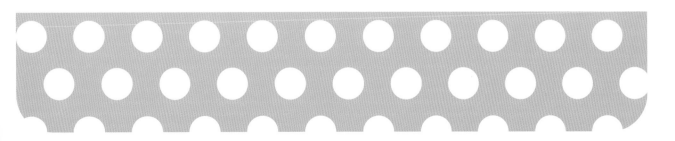

Black Olive Bread

Preparation Time 40 minutes, plus rising • Cooking Time 30–35 minutes • Makes 2 loaves •
Per Serving 600 calories, 21g fat (3g saturated), 97g carbohydrates, 3,800mg sodium • Dairy Free • Easy

²⁄₃ **cup lukewarm water**

2 teaspoons active dry yeast

3½ cups white bread flour, plus extra to dust

¾ **cup warm water**

2 teaspoons coarse salt, plus extra to sprinkle

⅓ **cup extra virgin olive oil, plus extra to grease**

½ **cup ripe black olives, pitted and chopped**

1. Put the lukewarm water into a heatproof bowl, stir in the yeast, and let sit for 10 minutes or until foamy. Put the flour, salt, yeast mixture, the warm water, and 2 tablespoons of olive oil into a bowl or a food processor. Mix, using a wooden spoon or the dough hook, for 2–3 minutes to make a soft smooth dough.

2. Put the dough into a lightly oiled bowl, cover with oiled plastic wrap, and let sit in a warm place for 45 minutes or until doubled in size. Punch the dough to knock out the air, and then knead on a lightly floured work surface for 1 minute. Add the olives and knead until combined.

3. Divide in half, shape into rectangles, and put into two greased loaf pans, each about 10 × 6 inches. Cover with plastic wrap and let sit in a warm place for 1 hour or until the dough is puffy.

4. Preheat the oven to 400°F. Press your finger into the dough 12 times, drizzle 2 tablespoons of oil over the surface, and sprinkle with salt. Bake for 30–35 minutes, until golden. Drizzle with the remaining oil. Slice and serve warm.

Grilled Garlic Bread

Preparation Time 5 minutes • Cooking Time 5–6 minutes • Serves 8 • Per Serving 400 calories, 20g fat (11g saturated), 50g carbohydrates, 1,600mg sodium • Easy

1 large crusty loaf
¾ cup (1½ sticks) butter, cubed
3 garlic cloves, crushed
a bunch of stiff-stemmed fresh
**   thyme sprigs**
salt and ground black pepper

1. Cut the bread into ¾-inch-thick slices.

2. Put the butter and garlic into a small metal or heatproof dish and set it on the barbecue grill. Let the butter melt. Season with salt and black pepper.

3. Dip the thyme into the melted butter and use it to brush one side of each slice of bread. Put the slices, buttered side down, on the barbecue grill. Cook for 1–2 minutes, until crisp and golden brown. Brush the uppermost sides with the remaining butter, turn over, and cook the other side. Serve immediately.

Corn Bread

Preparation Time 5 minutes • Cooking Time 25–30 minutes • Serves 8 • Per Serving 229 calories, 8g fat (1g saturated), 33g carbohydrates, 1,300mg sodium • Easy

oil to grease
1 cup all-purpose flour
1 cup cornmeal
1 tablespoon baking powder
1 tablespoon sugar
½ teaspoon salt
1¼ cups buttermilk, or equal
   quantities of plain yogurt and
   milk, mixed together
2 large eggs
¼ cup extra virgin olive oil

1. Preheat the oven to 400°F. Generously grease an 8-inch-square shallow baking pan.

2. Put the flour into a large bowl. Add the cornmeal, baking powder, sugar, and salt. Make a well in the center and pour in the buttermilk or yogurt-and-milk mixture. Add the eggs and olive oil and stir together until evenly mixed.

3. Pour into the pan and bake for 25–30 minutes, until firm to the touch. Insert a toothpick into the center—if it comes out clean, then the cornbread is done.

4. Let the cornbread rest in the pan for 5 minutes. Then turn out and cut into chunky triangles. Serve warm with butter.

White and Dark Chocolate Cookies

Preparation Time 15 minutes, plus chilling • Cooking Time 10–12 minutes, plus cooling • Makes 26 •
Per Cookie 133 calories, 7g fat (4g saturated), 17g carbohydrates, 100mg sodium • Easy

½ cup (1 stick) unsalted butter,
    softened, plus extra to grease
½ cup sugar
2 large eggs, beaten
2 teaspoons vanilla extract
1¾ cups all-purpose flour
1¾ teaspoons baking powder
finely grated zest of 1 orange
4 ounces white chocolate,
    coarsely chopped
4 ounces good-quality semisweet
    chocolate, coarsely chopped

1. Preheat the oven to 350°F.
Lightly grease three baking sheets.

2. Cream the butter and sugar
together until the mixture is pale
and fluffy. Gradually beat in the
eggs and vanilla extract. Sift in the
flour and baking powder. Then add
the orange zest and sprinkle in the
white and semisweet chocolates.
Mix the dough together with your
hands. Knead lightly. Then wrap in
plastic wrap and chill for at least
30 minutes.

3. Divide the mixture into 26 pieces
and roll each into a ball. Using a
dampened frosting spatula, flatten
each ball slightly to make a disk.
Put on the prepared baking sheets,
spaced well apart.

4. Bake for 10–12 minutes, until
golden brown. Let rest on the
baking sheets for 5 minutes, and
then transfer to a wire rack to cool
completely.

TO STORE
Store in an airtight container.
They will keep for up to one week.

Pecan Raisin Cookies

Preparation Time 15 minutes • Cooking Time 12–15 minutes, plus cooling • Makes 20 • Per Cookie 276 calories, 18g fat (7g saturated), 27g carbohydrates, 200mg sodium • Easy

1 cup (2 sticks) unsalted butter, at room temperature, plus extra to grease
1 cup packed light brown sugar
2 medium eggs, lightly beaten
1½ cups pecan nut halves
2⅛ cups self-rising flour, sifted
¼ teaspoon baking powder
¾ cup golden raisins
2 tablespoons maple syrup

1. Preheat the oven to 375°F. Lightly grease four baking sheets.

2. Cream the butter and sugar together until the mixture is pale and fluffy. Gradually beat in the eggs until thoroughly combined.

3. Put 20 pecan nut halves to one side. Coarsely chop the rest and fold into the mixture with the flour, baking powder, golden raisins, and syrup.

4. Roll the mixture into 20 balls and place them, spaced well apart, onto the prepared baking sheets. Using a dampened frosting spatula, flatten the cookies, and top each with a half pecan.

5. Bake for 12–15 minutes until pale golden. Leave on the baking sheets for 5 minutes, and then transfer to a wire rack to cool completely.

TO STORE
Store in an airtight container. They will keep for up to one week.

FREEZING TIP
To freeze Complete the recipe to the end of step 4. Then open-freeze a tray of unbaked cookies. When frozen, pack into bags or containers, and freeze for up to three months. To use Cook from frozen for 18–20 minutes.

Chocolate and Pistachio Biscotti

Preparation Time 15 minutes • Cooking Time about 1 hour, plus cooling • Makes 30 • Per Cookie 152 calories, 7g fat (3g saturated), 20g carbohydrates, 200mg sodium • Easy

3¼ cups all-purpose flour, sifted
3¼ cups unsweetened cocoa
  powder, sifted
1 teaspoon baking powder
¼ cup semisweet chocolate chips
1 cup shelled pistachio nuts
a pinch of salt
6 tablespoons unsalted butter,
  softened
1 cup granulated sugar
2 extra-large eggs, beaten
1 tablespoon confectioners' sugar

1. Preheat the oven to 350°F. Line a large baking sheet with parchment paper.

2. Mix the flour with the cocoa powder, baking powder, chocolate chips, pistachio nuts, and salt. Using an electric mixer, beat the butter and granulated sugar together until light and fluffy. Gradually beat in the eggs.

3. Stir the dry ingredients into the mixture until it forms a stiff dough. With floured hands, shape the dough into two slightly flattened logs, each about 12 × 2 inches. Sprinkle with the confectioners' sugar. Put the logs onto the prepared baking sheet and bake for 40–45 minutes, until they are slightly firm to the touch.

4. Let the logs rest on the baking sheet for 10 minutes. Then cut diagonally into 15 slices, ¾ inch thick. Arrange them, cut side down, on the baking sheet, and bake again for 15 minutes or until crisp. Cool on a wire rack.

TO STORE
Store in an airtight container. They will keep for up to one month.

TRY SOMETHING DIFFERENT
Cranberry, Hazelnut, and Orange Biscotti
Increase the flour to 2⅔ cups, omit the cocoa powder, and add the grated zest of 1 orange. Replace the chocolate chips with dried cranberries and the pistachios with chopped blanched hazelnuts.

Almond Macaroons

Preparation Time 10 minutes • Cooking Time 12–15 minutes, plus cooling • Makes 22 • Per Cookie 86 calories, 6g fat (1g saturated), 7g carbohydrates, 0mg sodium • Gluten Free • Dairy Free • Easy

2 large egg whites
½ cup superfine sugar
1⅓ cups ground almonds (almond meal)
¼ teaspoon almond extract
22 blanched almonds

1. Preheat the oven to 350°F. Line two baking sheets with parchment paper. Whisk the egg whites in a clean, grease-free bowl until stiff peaks form. Gradually whisk in the superfine sugar, a little at a time, until the mixture is thick and glossy. Gently stir in the ground almonds and almond extract.

2. Spoon teaspoonfuls of the mixture onto the prepared baking sheets, spacing them slightly apart. Press an almond into the center of each one and bake in the oven for 12–15 minutes, until just golden and firm to the touch.

3. Let rest on the baking sheets for 10 minutes, and then transfer to wire racks to cool completely. On cooling, these cookies have a soft, chewy center; they harden up after a few days.

TO STORE
Store in airtight containers. They will keep for up to one week.

Double-Chocolate Brownies

Preparation Time 15 minutes • Cooking Time 20–25 minutes, plus cooling • Cuts into 16 brownies •
Per Brownie 352 calories, 25g fat (13g saturated), 29g carbohydrates, 300mg sodium • Easy

1 cup (2 sticks) unsalted butter,
    plus extra to grease
8 ounces good-quality semisweet
    chocolate, broken into pieces
4 ounces white chocolate,
    broken into pieces
4 large eggs
1 cup packed light brown sugar
1 teaspoon vanilla extract
½ cup all-purpose flour, sifted
¼ teaspoon baking powder
1 tablespoon unsweetened cocoa
    powder, sifted, plus extra to dust
⅔ cup pecan nuts, chopped
a pinch of salt
a little confectioners' sugar to dust

1. Preheat the oven to 400°F. Grease an 8-inch-square shallow cake pan and line the bottom with parchment paper. Melt the butter and semisweet chocolate in a double boiler or a heatproof bowl set over a saucepan of gently simmering water. Make sure the bottom of the bowl doesn't touch the water. Set aside the melted chocolate.

2. In a clean double boiler or separate bowl, melt the white chocolate as in step 1 above, and then set side.

3. Put the eggs into a separate large bowl. Add the brown sugar and vanilla extract, and beat together until the mixture is pale and thick.

4. Add the flour, baking powder, cocoa powder, pecan nuts, and a pinch of salt to the bowl. Then carefully pour in the semisweet chocolate mixture. Using a large metal spoon, gently fold the ingredients together to make a smooth batter—if you fold it too roughly, the chocolate will seize and become unusable.

5. Pour the brownie mixture into the prepared pan. Spoon dollops of the white chocolate over the brownie mixture, and then swirl a toothpick through it several times to create a marbled effect.

6. Bake for 20–25 minutes. The brownies should be fudgy inside and the top should be cracked and crispy. Let cool in the pan.

7. Transfer the brownies to a board and cut into 16 individual squares. To serve, dust with a little confectioners' sugar and cocoa powder.

TRY SOMETHING DIFFERENT
Try making these brownies without butter. The recipe will still work, but you'll need to eat the brownies within an hour of taking them out of the oven—fat is what makes cakes moist and allows for them to be stored.

TO STORE
Complete the recipe to the end of step 6. Then store in an airtight container. The mixture will keep for up to one week. Complete the recipe to serve.

Sticky Lemon Polenta Cake

Preparation Time 10 minutes • Cooking Time 1 hour, plus cooling • Cuts into 12 slices • Per Slice 220 calories, 7g fat (3g saturated), 37g carbohydrates, 100mg sodium • Gluten Free • A Little Effort

4 tablespoons unsalted butter, softened, plus extra to grease

3 lemons

1¼ cups granulated sugar

1½ cups instant polenta

1 teaspoon wheat-free baking powder

2 extra-large eggs

¼ cup low-fat milk

2 tablespoons plain yogurt

2 tablespoons poppy seeds

⅔ cup water

1. Preheat the oven to 350°F. Lightly grease a 9 x 5 x 3-inch loaf pan and line the bottom with parchment paper.

2. Grate the zest of 1 lemon and put into a food processor with the butter, 1 cup of sugar, the polenta, baking powder, eggs, milk, yogurt, and poppy seeds. Process until smooth. Spoon the batter into the prepared pan and level the surface. Bake for 55 minutes to 1 hour, until a toothpick inserted into the center comes out clean. Let cool in the pan for 10 minutes.

3. Next, make a syrup. Squeeze the juice from the zested lemon plus 1 more lemon. Thinly slice the third lemon. Put the lemon juice into a saucepan with the remaining sugar and the water. Add the lemon slices, bring to a boil, and simmer for about 10 minutes or until syrupy. Remove the pan from the heat and let cool for 5 minutes. Remove the lemon slices from the syrup and set aside.

4. Slide a knife around the edge of the cake and turn it out onto a serving plate. Pierce the cake in several places with a toothpick, spoon the syrup over it, and decorate with the lemon slices.

TO STORE

Wrap in plastic wrap and store in an airtight container. It will keep for up to three days.

Blackberry and Cinnamon Yogurt Loaf

Preparation Time 15 minutes • Cooking Time 55 minutes, plus cooling • Cuts into 8 slices • Per Slice 287 calories, 15g fat (3g saturated), 35g carbohydrates, 100mg sodium • Easy

½ cup sunflower oil, plus extra
    to grease
1¼ cups all-purpose flour
1½ teaspoons baking powder
1½ teaspoons ground cinnamon
1⅓ cups frozen blackberries
½ cup granulated sugar
grated zest and juice of 1 lemon
½ cup Greek yogurt
3 large eggs, beaten
confectioners' sugar to dust

1. Preheat the oven to 375°F. Grease a 9 x 5 x 3-inch loaf pan and line the bottom with parchment paper.

2. Sift the flour, baking powder, and cinnamon into a bowl. Then add the frozen berries, and toss to coat. Make a well in the center.

3. In another bowl, beat together the granulated sugar, oil, lemon zest and juice, yogurt, and eggs. Pour into the well in the flour mixture and stir until combined.

4. Spoon the batter into the prepared pan, level the surface, and bake for 55 minutes or until a toothpick inserted into the center comes out clean (if necessary, cover lightly with aluminum foil to prevent it from overbrowning). Let it cool in the pan. Remove from the pan and dust with confectioners' sugar to serve.

TO STORE
Store in an airtight container. It will keep for up to two days.

TRY SOMETHING DIFFERENT
Apple and Cinnamon Yogurt Loaf
Replace the blackberries with 2 small Pippin or Braeburn apples, peeled, cored, and chopped.

Raspberry and White Chocolate Yogurt Loaf
Omit the ground cinnamon. Replace the blackberries with 1 cup frozen raspberries and 4 ounces chopped white chocolate, and use orange zest and juice instead of lemon.

Carrot Cake

Preparation Time 30 minutes • Cooking Time about 1 hour, plus cooking • Cuts into 15 squares •
Per Square 399 calories, 25g fat (13g saturated), 41g carbohydrates, 400mg sodium • Easy

½ cup (1 stick) unsalted butter,
   chopped, plus extra to grease
1 cup shredded carrot
½ cup golden raisins
⅔ cup chopped dried dates
⅔ cup dried coconut
1 teaspoon ground cinnamon
½ teaspoon freshly grated nutmeg
1 cup maple syrup
⅔ cup apple juice
zest and juice of 2 oranges
1⅔ cups whole-wheat flour, sifted
2 teaspoons baking soda
1½ teaspoons baking powder
1¼ cups walnut pieces

FOR THE TOPPING
pared zest from ½ orange
¾ cup cream cheese
¾ cup crème fraîche
2 tablespoons confectioners' sugar
1 teaspoon vanilla extract

1. Preheat the oven to 375°F. Grease a 9-inch-square cake pan and line with parchment paper.

2. Put the butter, carrots, golden raisins, dates, coconut, spices, syrup, apple juice, and orange zest and juice into a large saucepan. Cover and bring to a boil. Then cook for 5 minutes. Transfer to a bowl and let cool.

3. Put the flour, baking soda, baking powder, and walnuts into a large bowl and stir together. Add the cooled carrot mixture and stir well. Spoon the mixture into the prepared pan and level the surface.

4. Bake for 45–60 minutes until firm. Let cool in the pan for 10 minutes, and then turn out onto a wire rack to cool completely.

5. To make the topping, finely slice the orange zest. Put the cream cheese, crème fraîche, confectioners' sugar, and vanilla into a bowl and stir with a spatula. Spread over the cake and top with the zest. Cut into 15 squares to serve.

TO STORE
Store in an airtight container. It will keep for up to five days.

Index